RE

MW00881846

"I think this [book] is really going to open people's eyes to the suffering and the power to change that only comes from God to transform lives and communities forever."

Kelly Mamrick,
Friend Preparing For Missions

"Your first book was good (very good!), but this new manuscript is terrific! I'm praying that God will multiply its outreach to millions to recognize God's true identity - and our true identity in Christ – as More Than Conquerors! ...

"I believe this book should become required reading for missions classes - actually, for all church leadership classes."

Rick Deighton,
Minister, Professor, Author,
Creation Apologist, Missionary
to the Ukraine.

"A MUST READ! We love the book.

"Your book is truly a valuable reference account of obstacles, victories, and applicable scripture for anyone considering going and serving on the foreign field: a must read! It is also a gripping testimony for others to know about the faithful endurance of those serving Christ even when the 'roar' of Satan is ever present. Your narrative of God's work in the Philippines demonstrates how, through God's servants, He has truly overcome the enemy."

Daniel P. Beaver
Director of Boracay and
Panay Island Ministries,
First Love International

THE
ENEMY IS ROARING
AND THE
LORD IS BLESSING

THE
ENEMY IS ROARING
AND THE
LORD IS BLESSING

Steven Ray Bragg

Xulon Press

Xulon Press
2301 Lucien Way #415
Maitland, FL 32751
407.339.4217
www.xulonpress.com

Unless otherwise indicated, Scripture quotations taken from the New American Standard Bible (NASB). Copyright © 1960, 1962, 1963, 1968, 1971, 1972, 1973, 1975, 1977, 1995 by The Lockman Foundation. Used by permission. All rights reserved.

Scripture quotations taken from the New Living Translation (NLT). Copyright © 1996, 2004, 2007 by Tyndale House Foundation. Used by permission. All rights reserved.

Printed in the United States of America.

ISBN-13: 9781545632321

Dedication

This book is dedicated to the elders, pastors, leaders and their families of River Rock Church Philippines. They are wholly devoted to serving our Lord Jesus Christ, seeking the lost, and restoring wandering sheep. Their sacrifice of all they are and all they have is extraordinary.

ACKNOWLEDGMENT

I WISH TO THANK ALL OF OUR PRAYER PARTNERS AND financial supporters of River Rock Church Philippines. I want to especially acknowledge and say thank you for the Acts Church Elders for their spiritual wisdom and guidance.

THANK YOU

THANK YOU, FATHER GOD, MY LORD AND SAVIOR JESUS
Christ, and Holy Spirit, for allowing us to participate in
your Church. What an honor and privilege it is to serve
You. Thank You for Your grace and mercy, without which
we could not serve. Thank You for Your awesome Gospel
of salvation. Your faithfulness is steadfast and we are sus-
tained by it. Your church is established by it.

> *"For I am not ashamed of the gospel, for it is
> the power of God for salvation to everyone
> who believes, to the Jew first and also to the
> Greek. For in it the righteousness of God is
> revealed from faith to faith; as it is written,
> 'BUT THE RIGHTEOUS man SHALL LIVE BY
> FAITH'" (Romans 1:16, 17).*

Synopsis

"Be of sober spirit, be on the alert. Your adversary, the devil, prowls around like a roaring lion, seeking someone to devour" (1 Peter 5:8).

"The roaring of the lion and the voice of the fierce lion, And the teeth of the young lions are broken" (Job 4:10).

The ROARING OF THE ENEMY IS THE OPPOSITION WE experience when we enter a new community to plant a new church. His roaring has kept God's church out until we come in the name of our Lord Jesus Christ. Jesus turns each and every persecution, intimidation, and attack to our character and safety into blessing and success in establishing and protecting His churches.

We often repeat to each other Romans 8:28: *"we know that God causes everything to work together for the good of those who love God and are called according to His purpose for them,"* as well as the phrase, *"the enemy is roaring and the Lord is blessing."* It reminds and encourages us. We see it fulfilled time after time. Truly, with almost every mission, we experience the roaring of the enemy, but what always follows is the blessings of our Lord. Even the roaring works to accomplish the mission. He overcomes the roaring of the enemy that has blocked the way for many in establishing His Church: the fierce roaring that has keep His church from coming to each remote place.

Sometimes the enemy roaring is when we go to places with dangerous roads, deadly diseases, crocodiles, and snakes. Even witchcraft has been tried against us. The enemy roars in each of the lives of our pastors and church leaders. But we, through the power of Jesus Christ, conquer the enemies of sin, fear, doubt, persecution, disappointment, heartache, and loss. *"Who shall separate us from the love of Christ? Shall tribulation, or distress, or persecution, or famine, or nakedness, or danger, or sword? As it is written, 'For your sake we are being killed all the day long; we are regarded as sheep to be slaughtered.' No, in all these things we are more than conquerors through him who loved us" (Romans 8:35-37).*

SCRIPTURE QUOTATIONS

All scripture quotations are taken from the New American Standard Bible (NASB) except were otherwise noted. Highlighting and underlining of certain words of quoted scripture is by me for emphases.

TABLE OF CONTENTS

Short Stories of Faith and Encouragement

INTRODUCTION

"Be of sober spirit, be on the alert. Your adversary, the devil, prowls around like a roaring lion, seeking someone to devour" (1 Peter 5:8).

"The roaring of the lion and the voice of the fierce lion, And the teeth of the young lions are broken" (Job 4:10).

I AM A MISSIONARY SERVING OUR LORD IN THE Philippines. My wife Juliana, my son, and I arrived in August 2011. We plant new Christian churches in remote barangays (communities) and their associated smaller neighborhoods called sitios, made up of fifty to a thousand families. Many are accessible only by dirt road or footpath, or sometimes hanging bridges or wading across rivers with no bridge. They are often many kilometers from a town or paved road.

The remote barangays often consist of people who are malnourished and have little or no education and typically no healthcare. These are our target locations: where there are no other Christian churches. As of the end of 2017, we had planted thirty new churches. Of these churches, seventeen have newly constructed church buildings and parsonages, and thirteen are also house churches. We call these churches collectively River Rock Church Philippines (RRCP).

Most importantly, these new congregations are in barangays that have never had a church before.
Most heard the Gospel for the first time from us.

Each church has its own pastor who lives among them and teaches and loves them. False religion, superstition, and witchcraft are being replaced with the truth of God and His love for them. Hopelessness, prevalent in these barangays, is being replaced with hope. *"And this hope will not lead to disappointment. For we know how dearly God loves us, because He has given us the Holy Spirit to fill our hearts with His love" (Romans 5:5 NLT).* Thank you, Lord!

Filipino Pastor Alejo F. Alagos, my partner in this ministry, and I have coined the phrase, *"The enemy is roaring and the Lord is blessing!"* This is our experience. This comes from the verse, *"And we know that God causes all things to work together for good to those who love God, to those who are called according to His purpose" (Romans 8:28).* In all things – good and bad, success and failures – God is always working them together for His good and His purpose. God is sovereign and His purpose will always come to be. In fact, His purpose was predetermined before creation.

To set the background for our experience with our Lord's providence, here are some biblical examples.

JOB

Job is a good illustration of what I mean by the title phrase of this book. Job was a man of incredible wealth. His family was large and he enjoyed the good life of prosperity. Job was a man of faith with an extraordinarily close relationship with God. God knew his name and boasted about Job's faith in Him. This for me is the best possible faith: for God to know my name and enjoy my faith. Imagine that to be true for any of us. Amen.

In spite of Job's faith, or maybe because of it, he lost everything: wealth, family, and health. He lost it all suddenly and dramatically. Job's life was shattered and his faith was questioned.

While going through the trial, Job did not know it was a deliberate test of his faith. God Himself allowed Satan to test Job. Only God knew the depth of Job's faith. God knew Job would pass the test and both prove himself faithful and prove God's glory and sovereignty.

Truly Satan was roaring in the life of Job. *"Stay alert! Watch out for your great enemy, the devil. He prowls around like a roaring lion, looking for someone to devour"* (1 Peter 5:8 NLT). Job was taken to the limit of his great faith and survived the test.

Job's faith was under assault. In chapter 4 of Job, Eliphaz the Temanite tried to encourage Job in his enormous trial of loss. Although not all of Eliphaz's counsel was true or good, I think this encouragement was accurate. Eliphaz tells Job, *"In the past you have encouraged many people; you have strengthened those who were weak. Your words have supported those who were falling; you encouraged those with shaky knees. But now when trouble strikes, you lose heart. You are terrified when it touches you"* (Job 4:3-5 NLT).

Often, even with people of strong faith, when trouble strikes, we can lose heart or become terrified. I describe these times as *THE ENEMY IS ROARING*. It is when our hearts are attacked and we become terrified that the roaring lion is attempting to devour us.

Eliphaz goes on to describe Job's enemy, Satan. The enemy can only roar. He has no teeth. God is sovereign, and His protection and blessing are always available. By faith the enemy is always defeated. *"According to what I have seen, those who plow iniquity And those who sow trouble harvest it. By the breath of God they perish, And by the blast of His anger they come to an end. The roaring of the lion and the voice of the fierce lion, And the teeth of the young lions are broken. The lion perishes for lack of prey, And the whelps of the lioness are scattered"* (Job 4:8-11). Job's faith was steadfast. He was not prey. Satan's attempt to devour Job was to no avail. His faith proved authentic. The accuser was silenced.

The testing of his faith was indeed a life changing ordeal. The apostle Peter says these tests have purpose. *"In this you greatly rejoice, even though now for a little while,* *if necessary, you have been distressed by various trials, so that the <u>proof of your faith, being more precious than gold</u> which is perishable, even though tested by fire, <u>may be found to result in praise and glory and honor at the revelation of Jesus Christ</u>" (1 Peter 1:7 NLT).*

Fire: that is a good description. Peter calls them tests of fire. The outcome of the test is faith more precious than gold. Peter concludes, *"The reward for trusting Him will be the salvation of your souls" (1 Peter 1:9 NLT).* James says these tests build endurance; they are tests of maturity, or they lead us to maturity. *"We count those blessed who endured. You have heard of the endurance of Job and have seen the outcome of the Lord's dealings, that the Lord is full of compassion and is merciful" (James 5:11).*

The *ROARING OF THE ENEMY* was the testing of Job's faith. However, *THE LORD WAS also BLESSING.* For Job, the blessings of the Lord are his inspirational faith for those in trials even to this day. The author of Hebrews put Job in the category of faithful people and described them as *"men of whom the world was not worthy" (Hebrews 11:38a).* He is eternally honored in the Word of God that will never perish. Through his test, we get a window of observation into the glory and sovereignty of our God. In the end, Job also received a double blessing on what was already one of the most blessed lives.

DANIEL

THE ENEMY IS ROARING

The roaring of the enemy works toward God's purpose. In fact, it is a part of it. In the book of Daniel, King Darius appointed governors (satraps) over the provinces and then three commissioners over the satraps. Daniel was one of the three commissioners. Daniel was blessed by God and excelled in all he did. The other commissioners and satraps became jealous of Daniel and planned a political demise for him. They knew of Daniel's singular allegiance to his God and tricked Darius into signing an irrevocable law for everyone to worship only King Darius for thirty days. Of course, the man of God continued to worship only God.

Because Daniel only worshipped his God and not King Darius, by law, Darius was forced to feed Daniel to the lions. Darius's efforts to save Daniel were unsuccessful. However, King Darius hoped and prayed that Daniel's God was strong enough to save his respected commissioner. In their recent history, God had already proven Himself and He was well known to King Darius.

The enemy roared in the plot to kill Daniel. The hungry lions roared in their den. Daniel was shut up in the lions' den and the entrance was sealed until morning. The enemies thought they had won. The lions were about to have a tasty meal.

THE LORD IS BLESSING

King Darius prayed and fasted in the hopes that Daniel's God was true and strong. *"Very early the next morning, the king got up and hurried out to the lions' den. When he got there, he called out in anguish, 'Daniel, servant of the living God! Was your God, whom you serve so faithfully, able to rescue you from the lions?' Daniel answered, 'Long live the king! My God sent His angel to shut the lions' mouths so that they would not hurt me, for I have been found innocent in His sight. And I have not wronged you, Your Majesty'"* (Daniel 6:19-22 NLT).

God proved once again that He is God and there is no other. The lions' months were shut and no harm came to Daniel. As a result, King Darius sent out a decree. *"I decree that everyone throughout my kingdom should tremble with fear before the God of Daniel. For He is the living God, and He will endure forever. His kingdom will never be destroyed, and His rule will never end. He rescues and saves His people; He performs miraculous signs and wonders in the heavens and on earth. He has rescued Daniel from the power of the lions"* (Daniel 6:26-27).

Through the roaring of the enemy came the power of God revealed, leading to the destruction of the enemy. *"The king then gave orders, and they brought those men who had maliciously accused Daniel, and they cast them, their children and their wives into the lions' den; and they had not reached the bottom of the den before the lions overpowered them and crushed all their bones"* (Daniel 6:24). In addition, blessing came to Daniel because of his faith. *"So Daniel prospered during the reign of Darius and the reign of Cyrus the Persian" (Daniel 6:28).*

The result of the enemy roaring in Daniel's life, Daniel's unwavering commitment to God, and the resulting actions of God led to a governmental decree that significantly changed the law of the land. I can only imagine such an awesome event in my own life. God's reward to Daniel for enduring the test and standing firm in his faith was substantial. He was honored by two kings.

PHARAOH OF EGYPT

The same message is exhibited in the hardening of Pharaoh's heart against the Israelites. Everything works to God's glory. *"And once again I will harden Pharaoh's heart, and he will chase after you. I have planned this in order to display My glory through Pharaoh and his whole army. After this the Egyptians will know that I am the LORD"* (Exodus 14:4)!

The enemy roaring was Pharaoh's approaching army sent to kill the entire Israelite nation. The Lord's blessing was their great enemy destroyed in the closing of the Red Sea behind them. *"Thus the LORD saved Israel that day from the hand of the Egyptians, and Israel saw the Egyptians dead on the seashore. When Israel saw the great power which the LORD had used against the Egyptians, the people feared the LORD, and they believed in the LORD and in His servant Moses"* (Exodus (14:-31).

SAUL OF TARSUS

When Saul, who later came to be known as the Apostle Paul, persecuted the early church, the disciples were scattered and spread the Gospel everywhere: the church grew as a result. *"But Saul was going everywhere to destroy the church. He went from house to house, dragging out both men and women to throw them into prison. But the believers who were scattered preached the Good News about Jesus wherever they went" (Acts 8:3-4).* The enemy roaring was Saul going house to house to put Christians in prison, desiring to destroy God's church. The blessing of our Lord was the church spreading everywhere and multitudes saved unto eternal life.

The roaring enemy came again when Saul was on the road to Damascus, on his way to persecute the church. The Lord revealed Himself to Saul and blessed us all through the attempted persecution.

This violent man who put Christians in prison and had them murdered was shown mercy by the Lord Jesus Christ. The saving of such a man proved the unfathomable riches of God's mercy and grace. God worked His good and purpose even through the *"worst of sinners."*

"This is a trustworthy saying, and everyone should accept it: 'Christ Jesus came into the world to save sinners'—and I am the worst of them all. But God had mercy on me so that Christ Jesus could use me as a prime example of his great patience with even <u>the worst sinners.</u> Then others will

realize that they, too, can believe in him and receive eternal life" (1 Timothy 1:15-16 NLT).

The enemy roaring was Saul with letters to arrest more Christians in Damascus. The Lord's blessing was the demonstration of His great mercy on Saul. This is our example and encouragement even today. The now converted Saul becomes Paul and establishes the Lord's Church in Gentile cities. He then goes on to write a good portion of the New Testament.

JESUS

The enemy roared through the persecution and death of Jesus. The false trials, the approval for Him to be crucified, His suffering and death on the cross, and His burial into the tomb all appeared to be defeat for Him. It seemed the enemy had won. However, God was blessing as Jesus was resurrected on the third day, freeing us from death. His sacrificial blood on the cross purchased us all from the consequences of sin to eternal life and the magnificence of His love was fully demonstrated.

HIS GOOD – HIS PURPOSE

We love Him and He has called us for His purpose. Because we love Him, our lives are dedicated to His purpose. His good and purpose for my life are accomplishing His good and purpose. For us, River Rock Church Philippines, His good and purpose is to take the Good News to the remote areas of the Philippines: thus fulfilling our portion of the Great Commission. In doing so we establish His Church in each place we go. We teach His great command; *"And he answered, 'YOU SHALL LOVE THE LORD YOUR GOD WITH ALL YOUR HEART, AND WITH ALL YOUR SOUL, AND WITH ALL YOUR STRENGTH, AND WITH ALL YOUR MIND; AND YOUR NEIGHBOR AS YOURSELF'" (Luke 10:27).* We are intentional to always be in His purpose. This produces His good in our lives and ministries, we pray. His good is our good. It can be nothing else.

We often repeat to each other Romans 8:28 and the phrase, *"the enemy is roaring and the Lord is blessing."* It reminds and encourages us, and we see them fulfilled time after time. Truly, with almost every mission of our ministry, we experience the roaring of the enemy, but what always follows is the blessings of our Lord. Even the roaring works to accomplish the mission. He overcomes the roaring of the enemy that has blocked the way for many: the fierce roaring that has kept His church from coming to each remote place.

Indeed, as we approach a new place to plant a new church, the enemy roars with accusations against our character, intimidations to our livelihoods, and threats to our lives. Sometimes the enemy roaring is when we go to places with dangerous roads, deadly diseases, crocodiles and snakes. One time we baptized a family in a small pond only to find out later that day there was a six-foot crocodile in the pond with us.

Even witchcraft has been tried against us. The enemy roars in each of the lives of our pastors and church leaders.

However, we, through the power of Jesus Christ, conquer the enemies of sin, fear, doubt, persecution, disappointment, heartache, and loss. *"Who shall separate us from the love of Christ? Shall tribulation, or distress, or persecution, or famine, or nakedness, or danger, or sword? As it is written, 'For your sake we are being killed all the day long; we are regarded as sheep to be slaughtered.' No, in all these things we are more than conquerors through him who loved us" (Romans 8:35-37).*

This book features stories of Filipino pastors and churches who have met the roaring enemy and experienced the power of our Lord Jesus Christ as He conquered each attempt to harm us, thwart us , or scare us off from accomplishing our ministry of planting new Christian churches in the remote places. Our Lord is blessing each dedicated life and each church planted in His name, in His authority, and by His power!

> *"And Jesus came up and spoke to them, saying, 'All authority has been given to Me in heaven and on earth.*
>
> *Go therefore and make disciples of all the nations, baptizing them in the name of the Father and the Son and the Holy Spirit, teaching them to observe all that I commanded you; <u>and lo, I am with you always, even to the end of the age</u>'" (Matthew 28:18-20).*

STORIES

GOD IS FAITHFUL

Grace Chapel – Esparar – A Ministry of Planting Churches

"To open their eyes so that they may turn from darkness to light and from the dominion of Satan to God, that they may receive forgiveness of sins and an inheritance among those who have been sanctified by faith in Me" *(Acts 26:18).*

GOD CAN RESTORE

ABOUT A YEAR AFTER I GRADUATED FROM BOISE BIBLE College, I fell from the ministry. The old habits and addictions that I was in bondage to before Bible college overtook me again. For thirteen years, I wandered in darkness of sin and deprivation. Finally, I came to a place where I could no longer accept the consequence of my life. In desperation, I turned to God, asking if He could forgive such a one like me. I was 49 years old. My hope and prayer was that maybe God could restore life to me. Maybe He would provide some happiness to the later years of my life.

I prayed, but I had little hope. My sins were great. My life was dark.

Once I turned back to God, it would be thirteen years of recovery before I was fully restored to serving my Lord Jesus Christ. I not only had many addictions to overcome, but my guilt was strong. The enemy used this against me. The enemy was roaring in my flesh and my soul. Several times, I thought to give up and give in. What was the point of struggling to overcome sin if I was not worthy of any good or happiness? How could God forgive or even restore a reprobate like me?

THE ROARING OF THE ENEMY

The Roaring of the Enemy was my fall from the pastorate due to addictions and my lack of faith. He continued to roar in my life with doubt and guilt. I am sure Satan was certain he had successfully taken me out of ministry and service to my Lord. To my surprise and Satan's chagrin, God was not finished with me. He was to bless me with recovery, a renewed life, and an even greater ministry than I would ever deserve or even imagine.

THE LORD IS BLESSING

Our Lord sent pastors and elders into my life to encourage, mentor, and establish me once again in our Lord's service. Halfway through my recovery, in 2005, I was given $100. Based on the story of the Parable of the Talents, I was challenged to invest it in our Lord's Kingdom to see what our Lord could do with it. So I prayed, "Lord, this is your money. How will I use it to see an increase?" Like two of the stewards in the parable, I sought to invest this gift, as God would have me with His blessing increase it.

THE FAITHFUL SERVANTS

"After a long time their master returned from his trip and called them to give an account of how they had used his money. The servant to whom he had entrusted the five bags of silver came forward with five more and said, 'Master, you gave me five bags of silver to invest, and I have earned five more.' The master was full of praise. 'Well done, my good and faithful servant. You have been faithful in handling this small amount, so now I will give you many more responsibilities. Let's celebrate together ' The servant who had received the two bags of silver came forward and said, 'Master, you gave me two bags of silver to invest, and I have earned two more.' The master said, 'Well done, my good and faithful servant. You have been faithful in handling this small amount, so now I will give you many more responsibilities. Let's celebrate together'" (Matthew 25:19-23)!

I DID NOT WANT TO BE LIKE THE UNFAITHFUL SERVANT.

> *"I was afraid I would lose your money, so I hid it in the earth. Look, here is your money back.' But the master replied, 'You wicked and lazy servant...'" (Matthew 25:25, 26 NLT)!*

THE INCREASE - GRACE CHAPEL

At this time, one of my wife Juliana's sisters was praying for a chapel in her barangay. The people had no place to gather and worship. The Lord put in my heart to build a small chapel for them. We invested the $100 and others caught the vision as well. We all invested money and prayers to build the chapel.

Later the next year, we were on our way to attend the dedication of Grace Chapel: that very church. I did not know it was to become our first of many churches, or the ministry our Lord was preparing me for.

When we arrived in August 2006 for the dedication, everything was well prepared. There was a congregation assembled of the local people. Pastor Alejo Alagos, Brother Gaudencio Valdez Jr. (Jojo), and others had gathered the congregation for the dedication. Both Pastor Alagos and Brother Jojo were to become key leaders in the ministry that had just begun. The Lord had gathered His pastors. We were willing pastors, but it was still for our Lord to unveil His plan to plant new churches in the remote barangays that had no church, where most had not heard the Gospel of Jesus Christ.

THE CALL

When I arrived, I was still under attack from Satan, not believing that the Lord could use a sinner like me. Much to my amazement, once Pastor Alagos and then Brother Jojo learned I had graduated from a Bible college, they asked if I would move to the Philippines and teach the Bible. The majority of pastors were little trained in God's Word.

I wondered if this was a call from my Lord. Could God ask someone like me to serve Him again? With apprehension, I began to explore the idea.

The first obstacle facing me was that I had no financial support for the mission. It was financially impossible unless support was secured. None was available. It appeared that door was closed. In addition, my marriage was not ready. My addictions were still being brought under control. I still had relationships that needed to be repaired due to my fall. The question still remained if God could or would use someone like me. It seemed daunting.

All these closed doors were set in place to slow me down. The Lord gave me a glimpse of what could be if I stayed the course: if I allowed Him to prepare me.

I had to learn the true meaning of grace and mercy through my personal experience of their application in my life. Yes, God can forgive someone like me. The Apostle Paul learned about grace and mercy as one not only forgiven for persecuting the church but also appointed to help establish the very church he once hated and tried to stamp out through violence. The Apostle Paul put this experience like this:

CHRIST JESUS CAME TO SAVE SINNERS

"I thank the Messiah Jesus, our Lord, who gives me strength, that he has considered me faithful and has appointed me to his service. In the past I was a blasphemer, a persecutor, and a violent man. But I received mercy because I acted ignorantly in my unbelief, and the grace of our Lord overflowed toward me, along with the faith and love that are in the Messiah Jesus. This is a trustworthy saying that deserves complete acceptance: To this world Messiah came, sinful people to reclaim. I am the worst of them. But for that very reason I received mercy, so that in me, as the worst sinner, the Messiah Jesus might demonstrate all of his patience as an example for those who would believe in him for eternal life. Now to the King Eternal—the immortal, invisible, and only God—be honor and glory forever and ever! Amen" (1 Timothy 1:12-17 ISV).

THE TRIAL OF FAITH

Eventually, my addictions were overcome. In fact, I began teaching others the Godly principles of holy living to help them become free of sinful addictions that destroy the soul and prevent a complete life as a follower of Jesus Christ. Also, through Godly mentors, I studied the Bible afresh. The Bible calls itself the "living and abiding Word of God" (Hebrews 4:12 & 1 Peter 1:23). Through studying and teaching God's Word, my life was being healed.

However, God decided to take me through my greatest trial. This was a trial of faith. It built and established my faith: a faith needed for the mission work in the Philippines.

> *"You greatly rejoice in this, even though you have to suffer various kinds of trial for a little while, so that your genuine faith, which is more valuable than gold that perishes when tested by fire, may result in praise, glory, and honor when Jesus, the Messiah, is revealed"* (Peter 1:6, 7 ISV).

SATAN ROARED!

Like the trial of Job, I was to lose everything. My health and the health of my family stayed good, but we were to lose all our savings and the ability to support ourselves.

In 2008, when the US economy crashed, so did my job. It was a good paying job and we had become accustomed to the lifestyle it afforded. There were good jobs available in my field and I had a good reputation in the industry, but I could not find employment. Unemployment insurance helped, but it was not enough to meet our financial needs. I used all our savings and eventually our retirement savings to try to keep afloat.

About a year into this unemployment, I sent Juliana and my son to the Philippines. I feared that I could not feed them. I prayed their family would not let them go hungry. Unemployment insurance was running out. I continued to work minimum wage jobs when they were available. It was clear disaster was imminent.

I devised a plan to live out of my car: the only thing I owned. I was not able to make a house payment in almost a year and the bank wanted me out. The utilities were off and on as I was able to pay them. The utility company had emergency funds that were available and this helped. The little money I earned was just enough to feed Juliana and my son in the Philippines and me in the USA. Canned foods, bread and beans were my usual diet.

After two years, I came to the last of all my money and ability to support myself and family. I had a commission only job in my field. I had spent years training others to sell, but at this time, I could not do it myself.

One night after a sales appointment that resulted in no sale, I went to get something to eat while on the way home. I was down to my last $10, with no hope of any additional money coming in. This was the end.

The next day, I planned to start living out of my car. I had stocked some canned foods and Power Bars. However, as I prepared to enter a burger place, a man was standing at the door asking for money. I wanted to give him something, as was my custom.

I should explain that during this trial I continued to tithe and help others as I was able. Even if I did not earn any money in a given week, I would tithe whatever money I had left in savings. Whatever was in my pocket on Sunday morning went into the offering plate. My reasoning for this was to keep faith. In this way, I was recognizing that all blessings come from God. Ultimately, my welfare was His concern and my faith was in Him.

THESE VERSES DOMINATED MY MIND IN THIS TRIAL.

> '"*Seek the Kingdom of God* above all else, and live righteously, and *He will give you everything you need*. 'So don›t worry about tomorrow, for tomorrow will bring its own worries. Today›s trouble is enough for today"' (Matthew 6:33, 34 NLT).

> "*Bring all the tithes into the storehouse* so there will be enough food in My Temple. If you do," says the LORD of Heaven's Armies, "*I will open the windows of heaven for you*. I will pour out a blessing so great you won't have

enough room to take it in! Try it! Put Me to the test" (Malachi 3:10 NLT)!

My faith was enough at the beginning of the trial to know that if I was to survive, I needed God's blessing. When things got bad, I doubled down. I needed God and I needed Him desperately. Only He could be my help in this hour of need. I banked on His promises.

Meanwhile, I went in and ordered my burger, fries and a coke. It came to $5, leaving me with $5. I wondered if the man outside was still there; I prayed he was.

I rushed out the door, and there he was. I asked him if he was hungry and if I could I buy him a burger. He said yes and in we went. As I was ordering, this verse came to my mind: *"Do not neglect to show hospitality to strangers, for by this some have entertained angels without knowing it" (Hebrews 13:2).* Was he just a hungry man or an angel of God sent to test me? **Whatever he was, he was the final exam of this test.**

After we ate, I got in my car and started home. I prayed for my Lord to bless this man, knowing that after he ate, he had no hope for another meal. I prayed God would continue to bless the man. I also praised God that I had nothing to fear because He was faithful in taking care of me. My family and I have never gone hungry.

I Passed The Test of the Trial!
My Lesson...
GOD IS FAITHFUL!

As I continued to drive away, it hit me. GOD IS FAITHFUL! That's the lesson He wanted me to learn. Through this trial – this test of my faith -- it was imprinted indelibly in my heart that GOD IS FAITHFUL. Even though everything was falling apart around me, He is faithful and will take care of my family and me.

> *"For He will rescue you from every trap and protect you from deadly disease. He will cover you with His feathers. He will shelter you with His wings. His faithful promises are your armor and protection. Do not be afraid of the terrors of the night, nor the arrow that flies in the day. Do not dread the disease that stalks in darkness, nor the disaster that strikes at midday. Though a thousand fall at your side, though ten thousand are dying around you, these evils will not touch you"* *Psalm 91:3-7 NLT).*

We have always had a place to live and food to eat. I would need this unshakable faith in the Philippines.

"WINDOWS OF HEAVEN"

> *"Bring all the tithes into the storehouse so there will be enough food in My Temple. If you do,"* *says the LORD of Heaven's Armies, "I will open the windows of heaven for you. I will*

> *pour out a blessing so great you won't have*
> *enough room to take it in! Try it! Put Me to the*
> *test" (Malachi 3:10 NLT)!*

The next morning God opened up the *windows of heaven.* The doors that had been locked, opened. Someone left bags of food at my door. There was a check in my mailbox from a friend. I had not asked for money or food, but there they were. I was offered a job that I took. That Sunday, someone put a check in my pocket. It was for the exact amount I needed to bring my family home from the Philippines. The bank called me and we worked out a plan to save my home. After the bank rewrote the loan, the home I could not sell for more than a year now sold. I actually made a small profit: enough to help us move.

OFF TO THE PHILIPPINES

We began planning to move to the Philippines. After a year of working, we felt it was time to go. I was 62 now and Social Security was available. It was not enough to support us in the Philippines, but the desire to go was greater than we could resist. At the S.S. office, we discovered that our S.S. was double because our son was a minor. This was enough to support us.

Literally, I felt like we were in a birth canal. We were feeling the rhythmic pushes of labor. They became stronger as the time to move to the Philippines approached. The unlocked doors of opportunity were irresistible. I felt like nothing could stop us, and nothing did! We were being pushed into the birth of a new life: a new ministry. I had fleeting thoughts of "are we ready?" God was ready. He had made us ready. We had the foundation of what it would take. The Lord built on the foundation of HE IS FAITHFUL as events transpired in the mission of the Philippines.

THE DAY OF ARRIVAL

The next thing I knew, we were on a plane to the Philippines. This was a surreal experience. Like Alexander the Great, we had burnt the ship. We were committed and there was nothing to return to in America. Our home, our car and all our possession were sold. Only family and church friends were left behind. We arrived August 8, 2011.

One of the original locked doors to coming to the Philippines was where to live. Juliana had built a concrete block home for her mom and dad. Her mom was gone now and her dad, Tatay, needed care. We live in the home Juliana built and we are still caring for Tatay to this day. He is now 93. Along the way, we have been able to remodel the home with some American style comforts, like a flushing toilet and shower. No hot water or air conditioning yet. Thank you, God, for the invention of the fan.

MINISTRY CONFIRMATION

Just a few weeks after we arrived, Pastor Alagos suggested we launch another church. We managed to start three churches before we arrived with Pastor Alagos' help. Now I was going to be a part of our fourth church launch. Thank you, Lord, that we came with the blessings of enough money to launch this new church, which several people were supporting.

We rented two jeepneys, loaded workers from all three churches, and traveled to Esparar, Barbaza, and Antique. The workers from our three churches and local pastors that came to help went door to door, inviting everyone to a two night-Christian concert. There were about three-hundred people in all that came and listened. We played Christian songs and the teens put on interpretative dances to the Christian music as well as skits.

At the end of each night, Pastor Alagos presented the Gospel and called people to salvation and repentance. More than one-hundred came forward and gave their hearts to the Lord. We took their names and followed up. Three house church groups were formed. Eventually, they became a church and outreach center to more barangays. GOD IS GOOD! For me, this was God's confirmation that church planting was our mission. We were four churches now. Thank you, Lord!

THE ENEMY ROARED

The enemy roared when I fell from the ministry; when addictions overwhelmed me; when my reputation and respect from others and self were destroyed; when my faith collapsed and I ran to sin; when my life was ruined, in my estimation, without hope. I am sure Satan was roaring in delight that he defeated one of God's men.

GOD WAS BLESSING

God took me, in this self-imposed trial, to the outer limits of mercy and grace. I came to know the unfathomable riches of His love. *"In Him we have redemption through His blood, the forgiveness of our trespasses, according to the riches of His grace which <u>He lavished on us</u>. In all wisdom and insight"* (Ephesians 1:7-8).

I love that word *"lavished."* I picture myself standing under a huge waterfall with mercy and grace like water overflowing, the weight pushing me to my knees. They are more than I will ever need or even image -- available for anyone. It takes God's kind of love to forgive those who wander so very far from Him.

Because of my fall and restoration, my message to the Filipinos has greater depth. I know from experience the tremendous love God has for us. The sincerity and conviction from which I speak is real and authentic.

When trials come upon the church and its leaders and people, I can say with a doubt, "Do not worry: GOD IS FAITHFUL! STAND STRONG! GOD IS ABLE TO DELIVER! HE WILL NOT FAIL US!"

GRACE CHAPEL

Our first church is appropriately called Grace Chapel. When we named it, I did not realize that both my life and this ministry would be by and through God's grace and empowered by it. Our message is about His grace.

> *"But God is so rich in mercy, and he loved us so much, that even though we were dead because of our sins, he gave us life when he raised Christ from the dead. (It is only by God's grace that you have been saved!) For he raised us from the dead along with Christ and seated us with him in the heavenly realms because we are united with Christ Jesus. So God can point to us in all future ages as examples of the incredible wealth of his grace and kindness toward us, as shown in all he has done for us who are united with Christ Jesus. God saved you by his grace when you believed. And you can't take credit for this; it is a gift from God" (Ephesians 2:4-8).*

The Bragg Family

Esparar Church

Grace Chapel

THE POWER OF THE WORD OF GOD

Esparar ~ Calapadan And Pastor Jojo

"So that the proof of your faith, being more precious than gold which is perishable, even though tested by fire, may be found to result in praise and glory and honor at the revelation of Jesus Christ" (1 Peter 1:7).

PLANTING THE ESPARAR CHURCH

THE PLANTING OF OUR FOURTH CHURCH IN ESPARAR was not only a confirmation of our ministry, but also the beginning of my walk with God through the adversities and victories of church planting.

It is my belief that because we plant these churches in His name, not ours, these are His churches, not ours. We proclaim only His precious Gospel of salvation and not a church or religious or denominational creed. Only He receives the credit, praise, honor, and glory. That is why the roaring enemy has not harmed or thwarted us. Indeed, the persecutions are real and felt, but His churches are planted, people come to salvation, communities are blessed and transformed, and always our Lord is glorified.

We started this church with a two-night concert crusade. We now had three churches and were ready to plant the fourth. The three earlier churches -- Grace Chapel, Tabernacle of Praise and Hill of Zion -- were planted in partnership with our donors, Pastor Alagos, and myself before we arrived in the Philippines. I was instrumental in casting the vision to American donors and Pastor Alagos was feet on the ground and the expertise to start new churches. Pastor Alagos had trained the three churches in evangelism and inspired their hearts to save the lost.

THE ENEMY IS ROARING

A pastor was recommended for the Esparar house church. He seemed well suited. We had several meetings with him. I liked him.

In the beginning, all seemed satisfactory. However, as time passed, we received conflicting reports. Our visits there were clouded in mystery. After many months, it became increasing clear that the man we had set as the RRCP pastor for Esparar was not an honest man. He was not growing the congregation. He was receiving an allowance from us and only showing up sporadically. He was also scamming the people out of money: stealing from the poor in the name of Jesus and RRCP. He had deceived us.

The new church's first impression of RRCP and the Lord's church was discouraging at best.

THE LORD IS BLESSING

However, the work of the Holy Spirit on the hearts of the people was enduring. After we let the fraudulent man go, Pastor Alagos and I began to visit monthly. The people were forgiving and patient.

Always the question was when we would build the church building for worship. We were meeting in homes. This was our first experience with what was to become a ministry of house churches as outreach. Some of these house churches become large enough to build a church building, while others are in small communities where worshiping in someone's home makes more sense.

Esparar was to be a house church for about a year. We could not invest in constructing a building until they had a pastor.

PASTOR GAUDENCIO VALDEZ JR. (JOJO)

At the same time, Brother Jojo was considering leaving the El Shaddai: a ministry branch of the Catholic Church in Asia, especially the Philippines. They are mostly Catholic young people that feel a call to serve the Lord. The ministry was fashioned after the story of the seventy that Jesus sent out. *"Now after this the Lord appointed seventy others, and sent them in pairs ahead of Him to every city and place where He Himself was going to come" (Luke 10:1)*. And then also *"Go; behold, I send you out as lambs in the midst of wolves. Carry no money belt, no bag, no shoes; and greet no one on the way" (Luke 10:3-4)*. They were to carry nothing with them, living and serving by faith only. They depended on the hospitality and graciousness of the people they visit. The only thing they were allowed to take with them was a Bible.

They are little trained by the Catholic Church. Most of their training comes from discipling one another. I must admit, they are most talented in preaching, prayer, and worship. Their preaching and youth groups are dynamic. Because they are sanctioned by the Catholic Church, they are well received and the communities are very cooperative. The Philippines statically is 81% Catholic.

THE POWER OF THE WORD OF GOD – THE BIBLE

> *"For you have been born again, not by a seed that perishes but by one that cannot perish— by the living and everlasting word of God" (1 Peter 1:23 ISV)*

The El Shaddai preachers travel week after week, month after month, year after year, with only the Bible to prepare their messages and teachings from. As they read the living words of God, the Holy Spirit speaks truth to their hearts. *"For the word of God is living and active, sharper than any double-edged sword, piercing until it divides soul and spirit, joints and marrow, as it judges the thoughts and purposes of the heart" (Hebrews 4:12 ISV).*

Indeed, the Bible was written by the Holy Spirit. *"But know this first of all, that no prophecy of Scripture is a matter of one's own interpretation, for no prophecy was ever made by an act of human will, but men moved by the Holy Spirit spoke from God" (2 Peter 1:20-21).*

For many of the El Shaddai preachers, there comes a time when they realize they can no longer teach Catholic doctrine. In reading their Bible, they learn the truth and then need to decide what to do with it. Brother Jojo was such a man. He is a close friend of Pastor Alagos and they have had many discussions. Pastor Alagos came to a similar decision about his previous denomination and decided to join and lead our efforts to work for God alone. He was no longer hindered by his denominational creeds and politics. He was free to teach and lead as the Holy Spirit and the Word of God led him.

I am in no way putting down denominations. We all call ourselves something. To name oneself is by definition to denominate oneself. However, not all denominations are on target, just like not all church movements are. Sometimes we need to correct our path or leave it to walk a better one.

For Pastor Alagos, it was course correction. For Brother Jojo, it was a salvation decision. He was being *"born again.... by the living and everlasting word of God."* He knew he was called to lead in God's Church and now he found it. It was decision time. Pastor Alagos and I purposed not to offer a call for him to join us. If Jojo was to join us, we wanted that decision to be between him and the Lord.

Brother Jojo also came several times to hear me teach. At the time, I was preaching a series on Christian foundations called the *Essentials of Our Faith.* Soon after, Jojo decided to leave the El Shaddai, stepping out in faith. After he resigned, Jojo came to us and asked if we had room for him. We asked him to come to our monthly pastor meetings. Jojo was well known by our pastors. He was warmly received. Soon after, he joined us.

Jojo is a gifted man of God. He was the leader of the El Shaddai for our province for eight years. His understanding of the Bible is exceptional. Brother Jojo became Pastor Jojo. In our pastors' meeting, we learned that he and his family are from Esparar and the surrounding area.

The enemy roared through a dishonest pastor and a time of waiting. Esparar wondered if a church would ever be realized. I sometimes wondered myself. We had no pastor in sight. The enemy roaring in Pastor Jojo's life was his fear that all the people he knew, all those who followed him and trusted him, would now be disappointed in his decision to leave the Catholic Church and his respected ministry and leadership to join a Christian church.

The blessings were God preparing Esparar, RRCP, and Brother Jojo for a match arranged in heaven. The preparation and timing were providential. The Esparar church now had a pastor they knew and respected. They knew his family and they knew him from the El Shaddai. Pastor Jojo and his wife Concepcion's (Jiji) dream was to settle and pastor a church in their hometown of Esparar. God is good!

PASTOR JOJO'S HEART

Pastor Jojo's heart has always been for the remote and isolated communities of the Philippines. That was his ministry with the El Shaddai. After eight years of traveling the remote communities of our island of Panay, he came to know these communities well.

The remote areas are the poorest of the poor. Poverty, little or no education, superstition, witchcraft, no health care, and no medicines are the life of the people. For many in these communities, foraging in the surrounding forest and small gardens provides their daily food. They need the hope and blessings of God.

So many times, tears come to my eyes when I see their suffering. All of our pastors are dedicated to them. Jesus calls them *"the least of these."*

> *"Then these righteous ones will reply, 'Lord, when did we ever see You hungry and feed You? Or thirsty and give You something to drink? Or a stranger and show You hospitality? Or naked and give You clothing? When did we ever see You sick or in prison and visit You?' "And the King will say, 'I tell you the truth, when you did it to one of the <u>least of</u>*

> _these_ _My brothers and sisters, you were doing_
> _it to Me'" (Matthew 25:37-40 NLT)_!

We start churches that preach the Gospel of Jesus Christ and teach them to love God and to love each other.

> _"One day an expert in religious law_
> _stood up to test Jesus by asking Him this_
> _question: 'Teacher, what should I do to in-_
> _herit eternal life?' Jesus replied, 'What does_
> _the law of Moses say? How do you read it?'_
> _The man answered, 'You must love the LORD_
> _your God with all your heart, all your soul, all_
> _your strength, and all your mind.' And, 'Love_
> _your neighbor as yourself.' 'Right!' Jesus told_
> _him. 'Do this and you will live!'" (Luke 10:25-_
> _28 ISV)_

All that we are and do is summed up in that passage.

The Gospel of Jesus Christ, as well as our outreach ministries _Operation Kindness_ and _Operation Philippines,_ are saving and changing many lives, not only for eternity, but in the hope for today. In many of these remote communities, the look of despair on the people's faces and in their eyes is prominent when we first go in. It is heartbreaking that I have learned to spot malnourishment in the eyes of children.

As the church materializes in a barangay and we begin our Operation Kindness programs of feeding children, medical aid when we can, clothing, and scholarships for children so they can continue in school, the community transforms. Someone, in the name of our Lord, cares for them. Hope stirs in their hearts. We preach the Gospel pure and simple. Many are saved, and many consider. Lives are improved. Our Lord is faithful, hearing their prayers. As they learn to depend on our faithful Lord Jesus, their lives improve. In time, smiles come to their faces and hope to their eyes. Thank you, LORD!

Pastor's Jojo's heart matches our heart in this purpose and ministry. We are dedicated to sharing our Lord with them, helping as our Lord provides and watching our Lord and God transform lives and community.

BARANGAY CALAPADAN

Pastor's Jojo's late and highly respected father and many of his relatives are NPA (The New People's Army): a military rebel force. From time to time, they are very active in revolution. Some live in the safety of the mountainous areas of our island. Esparar and the nearby Calapadan are two of those areas. However, because of this, criminals flee there for safety as well. As Pastor Jojo puts it, even the sales people will not enter these areas.

Pastor Jojo and RRCP have been given permission to enter and protection in this area of Esparar and the sur-round communities. Calapadan is in the heart of one of the NPA territories. They have discovered that we really care for them. The leaders of the NPA in this area say we have the same goals of helping the people. Our feeding and clothing programs, along with sincere love from Pastor Jojo and Jiji, have opened the door for the Gospel. We now have a house church in Calapadan.

This is one of the churches where our Lord was before us, preparing our way. He has been decades in preparing for His church in Calapadan, and, we pray, the other communities of this area.

THE ENEMY ROARING

One enemy was revolution itself. Battles between the Philippine army AFP and the NPA have taken place in these valleys, making them extremely unsafe. Another enemy is the criminal element. It is still a present danger. Kidnapping and robbery are the way of the criminals.

As a result, the strongholds of the enemy are suspicion and fear of outsiders. When they see a white man like me, some may think CIA or ransom candidate. It may even be the same for Pastor Jojo, because of his association with an American church.

THE LORD IS BLESSING

The battles between armed forces are over now. At least for the time being, there is no need. Time and politics are clearing the way for the ambassadors of our Lord to enter. In fact, some of NPA leaders have retired, while others are in local politics. Our Lord's timing and peace are bringing the stronghold down.

Pastor Jojo's father was well respected for his legendary bravery. His uncle is a hand-to-hand combat instructor and a commander for the NPA. Therefore, Jojo and his family are held in high regard.

Also held in high regard is the life of Pastor Jojo. The NPA and community leaders know his life. They knew him as a godless teen smoking marijuana, gambling, and in trouble. When Pastor Jojo joined the El Shaddai, another reputation emerged. Over time, it became clear he truly believed in the God he proclaimed. He has never left the rural people he loves. His reputation as a man of God is unstained. His life is a true representation of his faith in the God he proclaims.

When Pastor Jojo decided to go to Calapadan to open a church, he had to wait for several weeks. His uncle, one of the nearby barangay captains, had to prepare the way for Jojo's safety. It was granted and the Calapadan church is thriving.

I have been there many times now, along with Juliana. Several pastors from the USA have visited Calapadan. Out of all of our house churches, these people show the most appreciation for us being there. Their love and respect for us is genuine. Our Lord is moving in the hearts of the people. They are receiving us warmly.

THE MIRACLE AT CALAPADAN

On one trip to Calapadan, we stopped at the barangay captain's home. Each barangay is governed by a captain and council members. The home, eight kilometers from a paved road, can only be traveled to by motorcycle and then by foot. After a long narrow path, there are seventy-two cement steps up to the first level. Then with a little walk, the view of the breathtaking and easily protected valley opens up. The valley is fertile rice land. The surrounding mountains are full of banana and coconut trees and various kinds of root crops. Chickens and pigs are often raised by families.

It is at this first level where I met the captain of Calapadan and his family. He has seven children: typical for a Filipino family. The captain's oldest daughter, Bebe, greeted us. A beautiful, smiling, and articulate young lady, she spoke English well.

As we talked, it became obvious she was educated. She had just finished college in Manila and received a Bachelor of Science in Information Technology. I was so happy that she would likely get a well-paying job and help her family. This is the Filipino custom. Families sacrifice greatly to get the children an education. If the children do well, then most likely they will help their family.

It was this way with Juliana. She is one of seven siblings. Their mother and father mortgaged land, worked hard, and tightened their belts to send all the children through college. Juliana was educated as a teacher. Soon after graduation, she went to work in Hong Kong. There she spent eight years paying off the family debt. She built a nice brick home for her mom and dad, who lived in a bamboo home before that. She also put three nieces through college.

When I heard Bebe had graduated, I had hoped the same for her family. In fact, the Petron Corporation in Manila hired her. However, as the story unfolded, it was also another typical situation for many Filipino families.

Bebe went to Manila for the medical clearance she needed to start the job. The clinic discovered she had rheumatic heart disease (RHD). Bebe was sick. Worse, the medication, which would be needed for a year or more, cost more than three times what the family would earn in that time. Without the medication, she would likely be too weak to work or could even die. Their hopes and dreams were crumbling. For most Filipinos, there is no health care or medicine. Oftentimes they can be diagnosed by a clinic but have no money for the healing medication. Even simple colds can turn into pneumonia without medication and be fatal.

They were now without hope. Only God could help. That is how I prayed. *Only you, Lord, can heal Bebe and bless this family. All human hope is gone. Only you, Lord, can make this right. Lord, bring honor and glory to your name and let the people know that you are God Almighty!*

After the prayer, I sensed something different about Bebe. My prayer for healing felt different. I felt an amazing closeness to God and her. Afterward, we held the morning service in Calapadan and then left for Esparar to have an afternoon service. My mind and heart were fixed on Bebe. I continued to pray for her.

That same afternoon, we arrived at Esparar for a worship service. I had not been there for almost a year. When I entered the church, a lady in her fifties kept holding my hand and speaking to me in Filipino. I could not understand what she was saying. She persisted in smiling and talking to me, not letting go of my hand.

I asked Pastor Jojo what was going on and he explained Pastor Alagna and I had prayed for her last year. I did not recognize her. A year earlier she had big red rashes all over her body and great sores. She was even losing her hair. She had been to many doctors with no help. Each monthly visit for three months in a row we prayed for her healing with no visible sign.

Well, this was that lady. I did not recognize her because she had no rashes. Her skin was beautiful, like a young girl's. God had healed her. I thanked God for the healing. Then I thought, *oh Lord, are you telling me something? Will you heal Bebe also?*

Well, rainy season soon set in. Calapadan is almost impossible to reach during the rainy season. We heard reports of Bebe walking to a nearby town. Normally, RHD would prevent her from walking any distances. We heard rumors only. We guessed that she had found a way to get the needed medication. Often, I would ask Pastor Jojo if he had been able to visit Calapadan or if he had heard more about Bebe. He could not reach Calapadan because of the rain.

Then one day after rainy season, we were coming home from a service in Anini-y. We dropped off the youth pastor and one of the youth at her home. The youth pastor ask if we could pray for the youth: she was dropping out of college because she had RHD. We prayed for her and then left for home. I mentioned to Juliana that it was the same disease Bebe has. I wondered if the Lord will heal them.

Just then, we received a call from Pastor Jojo. He had been to Calapadan. He was so excited he had forgot how to speak in English and asked to speak to Juliana. She became excited talking to Jojo. Finally, she got off the phone and told me Bebe is healed.

Our Lord had healed Bebe. She had an immediate healing. Bebe suspected her healing and had reapplied for the job in Manila. The same clinic that had examined her before now said there was no sign that she had ever been sick. Not a trace! She was cleared to work, and she is now working at the IT department of the Petron Corp.

We serve an awesome God! All praise and honor go to our Lord Jesus! Thank you, Lord Jesus!

THE PROVIDENTIAL WORKING GOD

I would like to accentuate the providence of God for Esparar, Calapadan, Pastor Jojo, and RRCP. It is clear to me that God has prepared our way for at least three decades that I can identify. I can only see a small portion of the picture. Nevertheless, this is what I recognize.

God made a way for His church to enter the Esparar and Calapadan communities. The first church in Esparar was founded in late 2011. Calapadan was established in early 2015. Pastor Jojo is opening two more communities as I write this.

Revolution had hindered the church from coming. There is now peace in the mountains and valleys. The NPA now protects our pastors from rogue elements. Only one of their own, Pastor Jojo, could earn their trust. Our Lord prepared the life of Pastor Jojo and Jiji to be the ambassadors of God the communities would accept.

POSTSCRIPT

Yesterday morning, I was in my bedroom in devotion and prayer. Actually, I was thinking about Peter in the upper room. God was preparing him for a trip to Cornelius' home to open the church doors for the Gentiles. God's hand was clearly working in establishing the beginning of His Church.

Just then, Juliana interrupted my thoughts and told me there was a man here to see me. I was not expecting anyone. I finished dressing and came out to meet him. I found a small older man sitting and waiting for me. He stood and introduced himself as the secretary of the council of his barangay. He came to ask me if we would bring RRCP to his barangay. **Amazing!**

Pastor Jojo was also here, working on our learning center. Pastor Jojo had talked to me about this possible church a few weeks earlier. The barangay is the most remote of the Laua-An municipality. Jojo said it is two tribes and they are "not very civilized." He wanted to go but was concerned for his safety. Nonetheless, he was talking to representatives and was planning to go there.

Now here sat the secretary requesting that we go. Jojo said he was at his house the night before, also showing up unexpectedly. Evidently, Pastor Jojo's uncle, the NPA commander, had contacted the barangay and recommended RRCP to build a church there. **God is in control!**

The barangay is an hour by motorcycle and then a two hour walk. I asked Jojo if we would build a bamboo church or, with tongue in cheek, a concrete block one. Jojo very directly said a concrete block. I asked how we would get the materials in. Jojo said they would carry them. The secretary nodded in agreement. Truly, the Holy Spirit has prepared their hearts and the way. **Our amazing God is in control!**

> *"Remember the things I have done in the past. For I alone am God! I am God, and there is none like me. (Isaiah 46:9 NLT).*

Yes, Lord, There is none like YOU!

Pastor Gaudencio Valdez Jr. (Jojo)

Calapadan House Church

Deliberate God—Part One

I Am Learning To Walk With God Without Fear, In Confidence That My Sovereign God Is Working His Purpose In My Life And This Ministry.

"For who has known the mind of the Lord, or who became his counselor?" (Romans 11:34)

"For My thoughts are not your thoughts, Nor are your ways My ways," declares the LORD. "For as the heavens are higher than the earth, So are My ways higher than your ways And My thoughts than your thoughts" (Isaiah 55:8-9).

INTRODUCTION

I WANT TO TAKE SOME TIME TO LAY A THEOLOGICAL foundation about the God I have come to love and depend on. The stories I tell of the ministries bear out the God we walk with -- the God who is sovereign in all we do and in each church we establish in Jesus' name.

I am learning to walk without fear, confident that my sovereign God is working His purpose. No matter what happens, if I am in His purpose, this life and the one in eternity are good. I share my observations and experiences to encourage you. What I have come to know about God and His working in my life is spectacular. I want to give Him praise and glory for the mighty things He is doing in establishing His Church in the Philippines through the ministry He gives us.

I. **The God I Have Come To Know**

> *"Teach me Your way, O LORD, And lead me in a level path Because of my foes. Do not deliver me over to the desire of my adversaries, For false witnesses have risen against me, And such as breathe out violence" (Psalm 27:11, 12).*

Our ministry is establishing His Church in remote places of the Philippines. In each church, we have met the roaring of the enemy trying to keep us out, discourage us from starting, and many times trying to destroy the church once established. Jesus said about His church, *"...upon this rock I will build My church, and all the powers of hell will not conquer it" (Matthew 16:18 NLT).* The rock that the church is built on is Jesus Christ and the confession of Him. *"...You are the Messiah, the Son of the living God" (Matthew 16:16 NLT).* Therefore, we build upon Jesus as the messiah, the Son of the living God. As a result, hell has no strength or authority over His Church. He will guard and protect His Church. I pray we continue to be and establish His Church and not ours.

As we establish His Church and I have fellowship with God, this is what I have come to know about Him. He is the Lord God Almighty, He is alive and powerful as revealed in His Word, the Bible. Pastor Dana Williamson said, after visiting the ministry in the Philippines, *"He is not a God locked in the pages of a book but alive, powerful, and active."* He does not change. *"Jesus Christ is the same yesterday and today and forever" (Hebrews 13:8).* He is the Creator of heaven and earth and all that has life. He is life. He is the I Am, the Alpha and Omega. He is the God of Abraham, Isaac, and Jacob. He is my Savoir and Lord: my God. He is the God I serve in this ministry. He is the God that goes before us, is with us, and surrounds us with His power and providence, all the while revealing His Glory!

OUR ENEMY

> *"The roaring of the lion and the voice of the fierce lion, And the teeth of the young lions are broken. The lion perishes for lack of prey, And the whelps of the lioness are scattered" (Job 4:10, 11).*

God's interaction with us as we move in faith is powerful, sovereign, and absolute. This is why the enemy can only roar: why he has no teeth. This is why we are victorious in what He has given us to do.

It is not a surprise that many times the greatest enemy we face comes from religious leaders and institutions. It was the same in the time of Jesus. *"Do you remember what I told you? 'A slave is not greater than the master.' Since they persecuted Me, naturally they will persecute you. And if they had listened to Me, they would listen to you"* (John 15:20 NLT). It was the religious leaders who persecuted Jesus. It was his people: even His own family.

There are some denominations in the Philippines who come against us they claim *"in Jesus' name,"* trying to prevent us from planting new churches and caring for God's people. Three in particular have tried to cause us the greatest harm.

One of them claims the baptism of the Holy Spirit with so called evidences of convincing people to vomit out demons and sicknesses. They claim angelic presences in their worship services. They claim the angels in their services are given the names of God like YAHWEH-JIREH: "The Lord Will Provide" and YAHWEH-RAPHA: "The Lord Who Heals" and so on. I believe the absurdity of this is self-evident.

Another denomination claims to be the largest Christian denomination in the Philippines. Yet they have targeted us and all their attempts have been overpowered by our Lord. They have claimed publicly that they will take over our churches, including land and buildings. They have sent imposter attorneys and impostor surveyors and have been caught falsifying documents. The enemy is cunning, but our Lord is absolute and sovereign. His will prevails! I have learned not to stand against them or try to battle them. If I do, then the fight is between them and us. Therefore, we give the battle to our Lord, and He is always faithful and overcomes the enemy!

I am reminded of the seven sons of Sceva.

> *"But also some of the Jewish exorcists, who went from place to place, attempted to name over those who had the evil spirits the name of the Lord Jesus, saying, 'I adjure you by Jesus whom Paul preaches.' Seven sons of one Sceva, a Jewish chief priest, were doing this. And the evil spirit answered and said to them, 'I recognize Jesus, and I know about Paul, but who are you?' And the man, in whom was the evil spirit, leaped on them and subdued all of them and overpowered them, so that they fled out of that house naked and wounded" (Acts 19:13-16).*

There are some people and even churches that claim the name of Jesus, but in reality do not know Him. When they try to exercise power over us, claiming in Jesus' name, it has in every case been reversed on them or they have been publically embarrassed. Some have even become sick.

A third, and truly the largest, most powerful of denominations is more covert. It is the Catholic Church. They attack us behind closed doors in politician's chambers. Another Catholic tactic, because they own the only cemetery in each remote barangay, is to refuse to allow Christians to bury their dead in the only available cemetery.

These denominations try to take our churches from us. Many times, just as we finish building a church, a challenge comes to take the building. We are well prepared for this. All our legal bases are covered and secure, but still the attempts comes. It is the enemy roaring without teeth.

As to some of their motives, the Apostle Paul said there are those who preach and teach from selfish ambition. *"Some, to be sure, are preaching Christ even from envy and strife, but some also from good will; the latter do it out of love, knowing that I am appointed for the defense of the gospel; the former proclaim Christ out of selfish ambition rather than from pure motives, thinking to cause me distress in my imprisonment" (Philippians 1:15-17).*

I pray what we are doing is of good will and love. I believe we are, and God moves with us, accomplishing all that is done in this ministry. If we were not attacking the darkness with the light of the Gospel; if we were not establishing His church in the strongholds of the enemy; if the lost were not being saved, then the enemy would not be against us, but would welcome us with open arms.

In our experience, the enemy has always been conquered and even humiliated. His Church and His Gospel have always been victorious. The Light, Jesus Christ, always expels the enemy's darkness.

"The light shines in the darkness, and the darkness can never extinguish it" (John 1:5 NLT).

"The people who sat in darkness have seen a great light. And for those who lived in the land where death casts its shadow, a light has shined" (Matthew 4:16 NLT).

"To open their eyes, so they may turn from darkness to light and from the power of Satan to God. Then they will receive forgiveness for their sins and be given a place among God's people, who are set apart by faith in Me" (Acts 26:18 NLT).

Indeed the enemy is great and powerful and he roars fiercely. He is not to be underestimated. However, our Lord is the Creator of all, He is the only God, and there are none who prevail against Him. *"Because the Sovereign LORD helps me, I will not be disgraced. Therefore, I have set my face like a stone, determined to do His will. And I know that I will not be put to shame" (Isaiah 50:7 NLT).*

Our mission prevails not to our praise, glory or purpose, but to His praise, glory, and purpose. These are His churches; this is His work: His harvest. We, to our surprise and satisfaction, are simply His workers in His harvest. What a privilege. Thank you, Lord.

II. **GOD!**

God is awesome, magnificent, glorious, supreme, sovereign and absolute.

HE ACCOMPLISHES HIS WILL

In every event or story in the Bible, God is causing the events, always revealing His power, will, sovereignty, and glory. Sometimes He does so obviously, while at other times He is more subtle. He is sovereign to work His will in each situation. *"Remember the things I have done in the past. For I alone am God! I am God, and there is none like me. Only I can tell you the future before it even happens. Everything I plan will come to pass, for I do whatever I wish"* (Isaiah 46:9-10 NLT).

"REMEMBER"

God has revealed Himself throughout history. When He acts, He is a mighty and powerful God revealing His glory and majesty. *"Remember the things I have done in the past. For I alone am God! I am God, and there is none like Me."* Indeed, there is none like Him.

CREATION

For me, the act of creation reveals just how awesome He is. Even today, science has not explored nor come to the end of understanding the boundless work of creation. It unveils His glory.

We see His love in creating a perfect paradise world, creating man in His own image, the gift of creation to man, His providential working in the lives of people and nations, His life on earth full of compassion and love, His contempt of religious hypocrisy, His demonstration of love on the cross, the power of the resurrection, establishing His Church, His infinite patience with the disciples, and on and on and on. We need to remember His providence, love, patience, and miracles in our own lives and the lives of those around us. REMEMBER ALWAYS HE IS OUR ONLY GOD: THERE IS NONE LIKE HIM!

"I DO WHATEVER I WISH."

I think most people object to these words. We want to put God in our box and have Him do or be what we wish. For instance, the Bible says that He is good: **"For the LORD is good: His lovingkindness is everlasting And His faithfulness to all generations" (Psalm 100:5).** And also, all His ways are just: *"The Rock! His work is perfect,* **For all His ways are just;** *A God of faithfulness and* **without injustice***, Righteous and upright is He"* (Deuteronomy 32:4).

OUR NOTION OF GOD

However, we want God to be what we perceive as good. We want God to be just, as long as it fits our notion of justice. We want God to be what we want Him to be.

This may be a key to why there are so many religions. Each religion has the god or gods that its worshipers want. Indeed, it may be a key to why we have so many denominations. Sometimes "theologians" stretch or ignore scripture to meet their personal ideas of God. They twist scripture and God to meet their own ideas of the church and salvation. Some interpret scripture based on their preconceived opinions about God, or loyalty to a teacher or creeds rather than an honest search for their Creator and loving Savior. Here in the Philippines, many claim the inspiration of the Holy Spirit, yet are completely ignorant of what the Bible says. They have little or in most cases no education or training in God's Word. Whatever emotion they feel or thought that comes to mind they claim comes from the Holy Spirit and act accordingly. Because they do not know the Bible, they have no way to verify if their thoughts or feelings are from God or merely their imaginations or desires.

UNDERSTANDING GOD

We cannot put God in our box. He is much too immense. We cannot understand God even minutely. As we study scripture; as we contemplate the workings of God in the lives of people in the Bible, people throughout history, or those around us and even in our own lives, we can begin to see God and understand Him. However, it is only from a finite discernment. The apostle Paul said *"Now we see things imperfectly, like puzzling reflections in a mirror, but then we will see everything with perfect clarity. All that I know now is partial and incomplete, but then I will know everything completely, just as God now knows me completely"* (1 Corinthians 13:12 NLT).

However, because God IS good, just, faithful, and righteous, He sets their standard. He Himself is the definition of these. If we judge these, we judge God: His very nature; His essence. Or worse yet, we become god, and define them and judge Him by our own standard.

As I share God from my understanding, I am, at best, understanding God *"partial and incomplete."* I am sharing God from my puzzling mirror. However, this is how I see God as one who walks closely with Him as a missionary in a life wholly dedicated to Him. I walk with God through trials, tribulations, and dangers. I walk with God in victories, joys, and divine protections. I witness His providence up close and personal in all I do.

I share God based on my honest understanding of God's Word, my experience with Him, and the leading of the Holy Spirit. These can never come in conflict. They must validate one another and be in harmony. There is only one God, one truth, and one purpose. In my walk with God, I pray to know Him as He reveals Himself. I leave room for error in my understanding of Him. However, this is how I understand my Lord. I pray what I have come to know about God will inspire you as it does me. I pray it will give you peace and confidence as you face life with God.

GOD IS SOVEREIGN AND NOT SURPRISED

Through serving in the Philippines, I have come to realize that, first, God is sovereign. He does whatever He wants. That is the reality and lesson of Job's story. *"Then Job answered the LORD and said, 'I know that You can do all things, And that no purpose of Yours can be thwarted'" (Job 42:1-2).* I trust His sovereignty. Second, God is not surprised. This is also what I find in my life and ministry. God knows what will happen from eternity. He knows every detail of my life and this ministry. He is not reacting to situations and then working it out to His good and His purpose. His purpose was established from eternity past, is now, and will be in the future.

More and more, as I experience the providential working of God, I come to understand there is no such thing as coincidence. There is only a divine orchestration of events established from before time and assured by Him as present events unfold. As God opens doors for something to happen, we see, in our limited way, how God has been working, sometimes decades, to the success of events that are in His purpose of establishing churches. I can see, since my birth, God's hand in everything and in all things. Even my rebellion was working toward God's purpose for my life. I see Him allowing me to be a part of His divine purpose. Truly, I see Him causing: not responding. Seeing this in my life and ministry is only a minuscule part of the grand scheme of His purpose and good.

The Enemy is Roaring and The Lord is Blessing

DELIBERATE GOD—PART TWO

God knows everything from beginning
to end in all its detail.
Nothing takes Him by surprise.

I. God Causes

> *"And we know that God causes all things to*
> *work together for good to those who love God,*
> *to those who are called according to His pur-*
> *pose" (Romans 8:28).*

DELIBERATE CREATION

SOME WOULD SAY GOD IS NOT DELIBERATE, EVEN IN creation. They say God sparked life and then evolution took over. This would say God is not powerful enough to create: to make something from nothing or speak creation into existence. It would also make much of the Bible false. Evolution becomes more powerful than God and more deliberate through the process of "natural selection." "Mother Nature" becomes their goddess.

There are some that say God created and then set things in motion: that the events of history are random and man-caused. Occasionally God intervenes, but in general, He is removed from time and history.

Some would say miracles are explainable in human terms, historical events, science, or superstition. Was there really a worldwide flood? Or only local floods restricted to areas where we find evidence of a great flood? Was Israel delivered through the reeds of the Red Sea in ten inches of water or did God part the sea and they walk on dry ground? Did Moses turn water to blood or was it red mud from a nearby volcano? Did Jesus really die for our sins and then be resurrected for our eternal life, or did He simply appear dead? Did the disciples revive Him from near death in the tomb or steal His body away in a great conspiracy?

Was it merely coincidence when Pastor Alagos, Edna, and I passed through without incident men who we were told would cut our heads off? Was my car radiator exploding boiling water on my face without burning me only odd or strange? Was late on a stormy night, Pastor Alagos' motorcycle mysteriously stopping just before a washed out bridge luck? Was successfully opening a church in a place that when tried years before resulted in death just a lucky break? Is this all strange or the providence of God?

Is establishing thirty churches in six years just good management or talented people? **I know it is neither!** If what we do here is in human strength, then my life and work are of no consequence. It would be temporal at best, or superficial. I would be better off relaxing in my retirement, sitting on my terrace in my rocking chair with a good book, reminiscing.

"EVERLASTING TO EVERLASTING"

"Before the mountains were born Or You gave birth to the earth and the world, Even from everlasting to everlasting, You are God" (Psalm 90:2).

"He has made everything appropriate in its time. He has also set eternity in their heart, yet so that man will not find out the work which God has done from the beginning even to the end." (Ecclesiastes 3:11).

God lives in the realm of everlasting. He knows the end from the beginning. *"Only I can tell you the future before it even happens"* (Isaiah 46:10 NLT). Because God lives in the everlasting realm outside of time and its limits, He can prophecy or tell the future before it happens in the realm of time. As an example, God gave, through the Bible, more than three hundred prophesies about Jesus. They are all prophesied with precise detail. Most were fulfilled in Christ's birth, life, death, and resurrection. The more than one hundred remaining will be fulfilled in His coming at the end of this age.

As an example, hundreds of years before Jesus came, it was prophesied that He would be born in Bethlehem; that He would be hung between two thieves; that His hands and feet would be pierced; that not one bone would be broken.

We cannot see beyond this moment. That is why we wear seatbelts -- right? We cannot predict the next second. God sees it all: knows it all. He knows and lives in eternity outside of our past, present and future. *"Praise the LORD, the God of Israel, who lives from everlasting to everlasting! And all the people shouted 'Amen!' and praised the LORD"* *(1 Chronicles 16:36 NLT).*

KNOWING THE END FROM THE BEGINNING - REVELATION

The Book of Revelation tells us the future: the unveiling or revealing of future events. The Apostle John wrote at the end of the first century with precise detail exactly what will happen in the end of our age. He wrote with careful description of the coming judgment and consummation of God's Church: His bride -- you and me. The revelation was given to him by the resurrected Jesus Christ himself.

As an example of God doing what He wants throughout time and eternity, God tells us of a future where this earth and heaven come to an end and a new earth and heaven are made. God lives with us in the new earth and heaven.

This event is predicted in the Bible several times throughout history. About three thousand years ago, the book of Psalms declared, *"Long ago You laid the foundation of the earth and made the heavens with Your hands. They will perish, but You remain forever; they will wear out like old clothing. You will change them like a garment and discard them" (Psalm 102:25-26 NLT).* Then two thousand years ago, the event is proclaimed again in the New Testament book of Hebrews. *"And, 'You, Lord, in the beginning laid the foundation of the earth, and the heavens are the works of your hands; they will perish, but You remain; and they all will become old like a garment, and like a mantle you will roll them up; like a garment they will also be changed. But You are the same, and Your years will not come to an end'" (Hebrews 1: 10-12).*

Then, about thirty years later, about 97 A.D., the apostle John wrote the Book of Revelation about the end of the age. *"Then I saw a new heaven and a new earth; for the first heaven and the first earth passed away" (Revelations 21:1a).*

God created the heavens and the earth. One day at the end of this age and the beginning of the new, He will discard them like old worn out clothing. One day we will be there to witness the event: in fact, we will be part of it. We will be at the predestined event, just like those who were there at the predicted and predestined coming of our Savior Jesus Christ. *"This Man, delivered over by the predetermined plan and foreknowledge of God, you nailed to a cross by the hands of godless men and put Him to death"*

(Acts 2:23). They lived at a time when more than three hundred prophesies in the scriptures were fulfilled.

MY POINT

My point is that God knows everything from beginning to end in every detail. Nothing takes Him by surprise. He is sovereign in all things. All things, all events, all life are by His will only. Jesus said not even the death of a single bird or the falling out of each human hair goes unnoticed by God. *"Are not two sparrows sold for a cent? And yet not one of them will fall to the ground apart from your Father. But the very hairs of your head are all numbered." (Matthew 10:29-30)* He knows the beginning, end and everything in between in complete detail. He either causes, works through, or allows events for His purpose.

There is only one God and His one purpose: His purpose. *"Declaring the end from the beginning, And from ancient times things which have not been done, Saying, 'My purpose will be established, And I will accomplish all My good pleasure'" (Isaiah 46:10).* Here is God's purpose and pleasure. *"God decided in advance [purposed] to adopt us into His own family by bringing us to Himself through Jesus Christ. This is what He wanted to do, and it gave Him great pleasure" (Ephesians 1:5 NLT).*

The deciding "in advance" was before the creation of the world. *"Just as He chose us in Him **before the foundation of the world**, that we would be holy and blameless before Him" (Ephesians 1:4).* He chose "in advance" that we would be Holy and blameless through Jesus Christ. God determined that the salvation of man would only come through Jesus Christ. Again, He did this before creation; *"before the foundation of the world."* Also, *"And there is salvation in no one else; for there is no other name under heaven that has been given among men by which we must be saved" (Acts 4:12).*

AS I UNDERSTAND IT

God's one purpose was to create you and me in His image and likeness, saving us from ourselves (sin resulting in death) via the sacrifice of Himself as the Word incarnate on the cross and the resulting resurrection, freeing us from death, and living with us in eternity.

We are His supreme (sovereign) good and purpose. Everything else -- all creation, all effort, all events, all that is predestined, and all predetermined -- serves only God's one good and only purpose: that we can have a relationship with Him now and forever. Our lives, if we love Him -- if we respond to His call of salvation -- live within His good and purpose. Our good can only be His good. I want only His good in my life. I believe my good, which is His good, can only come by living in His purpose. Amen.

Whether we suffer in trial, testing, or death, or rejoice in life, if we live in His purpose and will, then all is good. If I suffer, die, or rejoice outside of God, it is all for nothing. However, if I suffer, die, or rejoice in His purpose then there is reason, purpose, and good in all. I remember a movie line: "It's a good day to die." Or maybe, it could be said it's a wasted day to die, or, even worse, a wasted death and even more than that, a wasted life. We all live and suffer and rejoice and die. Will our life be within God's good and purpose, or will it be for nothing?

Now we can see more clearly Romans 8:28 -- *"And we know that God causes all things to work together for good to those who love God, to those who are called according to His purpose."* The good for those who love God is His good and purpose. When God works together for my good, it must be His good for my life. I want nothing else. I understand these as synonymous.

God is not caught by surprise, then arranging unseen or unknown events suddenly made known, to work out somehow if He is able or willing. He has purposed before the foundation of the world what will happen.

His will was established. His will is being accomplished. His will is ensured by Himself. He is sovereign. He is all present everywhere and at all times. He is all knowing. He is all powerful! *"Remember the former things long past, For I am God, and there is no other; I am God, and there is no one like Me, Declaring the end from the beginning, And from ancient times things which have not been done, Saying,* **'My purpose will be established, And I will accomplish all <u>My good pleasure</u>'"** *(Isaiah 46:9-10).*

ROMANS 8:28

If we love God and are living in His purpose, God is causing and working His purpose in and through our lives. He does this absolutely because He is sovereign and it is His *"good pleasure."*

Romans 8:28 is God telling us that we, in each of our lives, are a part of God's eternal plan. At the end of the age, we will either be in judgment and death because we lived lives of no consequence outside of God's purpose, or resurrected to eternal life with our loving God. If we are resurrected unto eternal life it is because we lived life in His purpose and for His good. Consequently, when He rolls up the dead, corrupted creation like an old garment and discards it, the new heaven and the new earth come and God lives with us there for eternity.

GOD'S GOOD IS OUR GOOD

You see, since before creation, in creation, through history, and specifically in our lives, *"God causes all things to work together for good."* God's deliberate purpose is that salvation is through His Son Jesus Christ. Also, His desire is that we would answer His call and become like His Son. *"For those whom he foreknew he also predestined to be conformed to the image of his Son, in order that the Son might be the firstborn among many brothers"* (Romans 8:29).

We can refuse God and His purpose or accept them. Every life, every life story, and each event reveal God working to bring us to discover Him or know Him better. We come to know His purpose of salvation. We come to know how our own lives work in His sovereign and everlasting purpose. God is causing His purpose throughout time, and in each of our lives.

God was not surprised when Adam and Eve chose to sin. The sending of the Savior was not plan "B". He knew they would sin and reject Him as God, even before the creation of the world. The process of creating man in Their own Image and likeness, sin and death entering our lives and the world, the sending of a Savior, the Gospel calling us to repentance: it was all predetermined -- ordered by God. God works and causes His will to be done, in my life and yours in all God has given us to do. The new heaven and the new earth are the culmination of the creation and salvation of man.

> Then I saw a new heaven and a new earth; for the first heaven and the first earth passed away, and there is no longer any sea. And I saw the holy city, new Jerusalem, coming down out of heaven from God, made ready as a bride adorned for her husband. And I heard a loud voice from the throne, saying, "Behold, the tabernacle of God is among men, and He will dwell among them, and they shall be His people, and God Himself will be among them (Revelation 21:1-3)."

CONSIDER JOB

A further illustration of God causing events for His purpose is the life of Job. In this story God causes, tests, allows, and ordains events.

In answering the accuser, Satan, God says, *"'All right, you may test him,' the LORD said to Satan. 'Do whatever you want [allow] with everything he possesses, but don't harm him physically [ordain].' So Satan left the LORD's presence" (Job 1:12 NLT).* Then later God allows and ordains, granting Satan even more power to test Job with his health. *"'All right, do with him as you please,' the LORD said to Satan. 'But spare his life'" (Job 2:6 NLT).*

Once Job's testing was finished, God reversed all the harm and blessed Job even more than before. God is good and just. *"When Job prayed for his friends, the LORD restored his fortunes. In fact, the LORD gave him twice as much as before!" (Job 42:10 NLT)*

The interpretation and application of Job's story is difficult at best. However, some things are clearly understood. God caused the testing of Job and allowed his suffering with limits and divine purpose. Satan was the agent of the testing and suffering. In the end, God blessed Job. God was sovereign and deliberate in all.

God was deliberate in setting up the testing of Job by asking Satan if he had considered him. *"Then the LORD asked Satan, "Have you noticed My servant Job" (Job 1:8)?* God knew in advance that Satan would accuse Him of bribing Job's faith with wealth and say that Job's faith was conditional on prosperity. This was no surprise to God. He knew the entire situation and the outcome. That is who Satan is - the Accuser. *"For the accuser of our brothers and sisters has been thrown down to earth—the one who accuses them before our God day and night."* (Revelation 12:10b)

DIVINE PURPOSE

Job's testing results, or God's divine purpose made known, are listed below:

- Satan came to know that Job's faith was genuine.
- Satan had accused God of bribing Job's faith with favoritism.
- Indeed God favored Job, but it was because of Job's faith, not to receive Job's faith.
- Job was faithful in both blessing and adversity.
- Job came to understand God in a greater way.
- You and I, as we examine Job's trial, come to understand God better also.
- Job's life reveals to us a window into God's nature and sovereignty.

> *"Then Job replied to the LORD: 'I know that You can do anything, and no one can stop You.' You asked, 'Who is this that questions My wisdom with such ignorance?' It is I—and I was talking about things I knew nothing*

*about, things far too wonderful for me'" (Job
42:1-3 NLT).*

THE HONOR TO DEFEND GOD

The testing of Job's faith proved that his faith was
genuine. However, more than that, Job's faith defended
the honor of God. Satan accused God of favoritism. He
accused God of being unjust. Job's faithfulness proved
Satan's accusations against God were wrong. Job's faith
was not the result of favoritism but because of Job's
knowledge of God and of his faithfulness as God's servant.
Job was a faithful man in prosperity and while suffering
need. Like a knight defending his king, Job defended the
honor of the Lord God Almighty. OH, TO BE GIVEN SUCH
A DISTINCTION AND PRIVILEGE.

When others see us in prosperity or suffering a trial,
will they see the God we proclaim? Will they see our God
as faithful, sovereign, good and just or will they see by our
action that we believe His is none of these?

DELIBERATE GOD—PART THREE

My Personal God

No matter what, we can trust Him!
We cannot help but trust Him; He is God! Amen!

FAITH IN GOD'S PURPOSE
TESTING OR TRIAL – LESSONS OF JOB

I HAVE FAITH IN THE PROCESS OF TESTING AND TRIAL.
I call these times "The Enemy is Roaring."

Satan roared in the testing of Job. I am sure he thought he had both God and Job over a barrel. When God granted him even more authority over Job's health, he must have roared with delight. *"Satan answered the LORD and said, 'Skin for skin! Yes, all that a man has he will give for his life.'" (Job 2:4)* Satan thought Job would relent in his faith in God to spare his own life.

The lessons here have many applications.

- God knew Job's faith and knew he would endure the trial faithfully.
- Satan came to know man can worship God because of love or faith, not simply for what he can receive.
- The relationship between Job and God was genuine,
- Deeper faith and greater understanding of God come through testing or trial.
- God has purpose and design in trial.
- Whatever the trial, God is deliberate, absolute, and sovereign.
- Better to stand strong in faith than to fold under pressure.

In each trial, we come to know even more that God is sovereign and faithful. No matter what, we can trust Him. We cannot help but trust Him; He is God!

This is why Pastor Alagos and I say to each other often *The Enemy Is Roaring and The Lord Is Blessing!* In addition, we recite Romans 8:28. We love God and we are in His purpose. There is cause and good in each trial. Even our trial is working God's purpose and His good. Our faith and prayer is that God's purpose and good is also ours. Each roar of intimidation brings purpose, good, and God's sovereign will. For us, our God-given purpose is to preach His Gospel and establish His churches in remote places of the Philippines.

"Who is there to harm you if you prove zealous for what is good? But even if you should suffer for the sake of righteousness, you are blessed. And do not fear their intimidation, and do not be troubled, but sanctify Christ as Lord in your hearts, always being ready to make a defense to everyone who asks you to give an account for the hope that is in you, yet with gentleness and reverence" (1 Peter 3:13-15).

For us, the result of the roaring enemy is God's blessings as we successfully deliver His Gospel of salvation.

- Lives are saved.
- Families and relationships are healed.
- His Church is established.
- Hope becomes real for the hopeless.
- The gates of hell have no power.
- Satan and his pawns are defeated and dishonored as they see the glory of God become evident.
- The children of God are revealed. Amen!

For I consider that the sufferings of this present time are not worthy to be compared with the glory that is to be revealed to us. For the anxious longing of the creation waits eagerly for the revealing of the sons of God. For the creation was subjected to futility, not willingly, but because of Him who subjected it, in hope

*that the creation itself also will be set free from
its slavery to corruption into the freedom of the
glory of the children of God (Romans 8:18-21).*

Through the adversity and evil we face in this corrupted
world, God reveals Himself as our Savior and loving God.
As we walk through the trials of life, our faith is made
known and our salvation is matured and revealed.

*"In this you greatly rejoice, even though now
for a little while, if necessary, you have been
distressed by various trials, so that the proof
of your faith, being more precious than gold
which is perishable, even though tested by
fire, may be found to result in praise and glory
and honor at the revelation of Jesus Christ;
and though you have not seen Him, you love
Him, and though you do not see Him now, but
believe in Him, you greatly rejoice with joy
inexpressible and full of glory, obtaining as
the outcome of your faith the salvation of your
souls" (1 Peter 1:7-9).*

EXODUS - JUST ONE MORE ILLUSTRATION OF GOD'S DELIBERATE SOVEREIGNTY

Exodus is also is an amazing story of God's deliberate sovereignty in causing events. God had arranged
that Israel would become slaves in Egypt. "God said to

Abram, *'Know for certain that your descendants will be strangers in a land that is not theirs, where they will be enslaved and oppressed four hundred years. But I will also judge the nation whom they will serve, and afterward they will come out with many possessions'"* (Genesis 15:13-14). Remember that God knew this even before creation.

God told Abraham that his family, through Isaac, would be slaves in Egypt. About two hundred years later, God arranged through Abraham's great grandson, Joseph, that Israel would settle in Egypt and consequently become Egypt's slave.

THE PROVIDENTIAL WORKING OF GOD THROUGH JOSEPH

The story of all the hardships of Joseph and blessings of God are no less than miraculous.

From the time of his first dreams to rule his family, to the pit, to being a slave in the household of Potiphar, then prison, and finally second in command of Egypt, God's providence was made evident. God maneuvered Joseph's life to rule with Pharaoh in order to bring Israel's family to Egypt to ultimately become slaves. *"Hurry and go up to my father, and say to him, 'Thus says your son Joseph, "God has made me lord of all Egypt; come down to me, do not delay"* (Genesis 45:9).

God also moved the earth's weather and climate to accomplish His purpose. God caused Pharaoh to dream about these weather events and their consequences. Then

Joseph was moved into place to be able to interpret the dream. As a result, Pharaoh appointed Joseph to manage the events for Egypt. The famine also caused Jacob to send his sons to Egypt to buy grain. Consequently, the trip to Egypt caused the reunion of Joseph with his family and the subsequent move of Israel to Egypt where they would eventually be enslaved for four hundred years just as God had told Abraham.

The Pharaohs that came to rule after Joseph enslaved the growing nation of Israel. God waited four hundred years to rescue them. When Israel's family came to Egypt because of Joseph, they were seventy in number. During the four hundred years, God grew the family of Israel into a significant nation. It is estimated by some that by the time Israel left Egypt, they were a nation of two-million to six-million Israelites.

When they left Egypt, they took all the spoils with them. God blessed their slavery to create a great and wealthy nation of God. God had told Abraham, *"afterward they will come out with many possessions."* Israel's slave labor made Egypt a wealthy nation. At the freeing of Israel, God gave that wealth to Israel. It was all predestined by God. Because God is sovereign, He deliberately made it come to pass. God moved people, events, and climates to accomplish His purpose.

THE DELIVERER

The raising up of their deliverer, Moses, to lead them out of the bondage of slavery was indeed another deliberate act of God. God created an irresistible beauty in the baby Moses that led his mother to spare him. It was God's hand in it all. Even the basket sent on the Nile River with the baby Moses in it was no accident. *"The woman conceived and bore a son; and when she saw that he was beautiful, she hid him for three months. But when she could hide him no longer, she got him a wicker basket and covered it over with tar and pitch. Then she put the child into it and set it among the reeds by the bank of the Nile" (Exodus 2:2-3).*

God ordained the discovery of the basket and baby Moses by Pharaoh's daughter and his raising in Egypt as her son. God deliberately acted to raise up a deliverer for Israel at God's appointed time, as He told Abraham about six hundred years prior. *"He has made everything appropriate in its time" (Ecclesiastes 3:11a).*

The raising of Moses in the household of Pharaoh for forty years and the shepherding for forty years in Midian were all the providential hand of God to prepare Israel's redeemer. *"Is the one whom God sent to be both a ruler and a deliverer with the help of the angel who appeared to him in the thorn bush" (Acts 7:35b).*

Finally, the appointed time for Moses to free Israel arrived, with God appearing from a burning bush. From the bush the Lord told Moses *"Now, behold, the cry of the sons of Israel has come to Me; furthermore, I have seen the oppression with which the Egyptians are oppressing them. Therefore, come now, and I will send you to Pharaoh, so that you may bring My people, the sons of Israel, out of Egypt" (Exodus 3:9-10).*

However, there would be delays and obstacles before Pharaoh would let Israel go. God caused all of the events through His hardening of Pharaoh's heart. *"But I will harden Pharaoh's heart that I may multiply My signs and My wonders in the land of Egypt." (Exodus 7:3)*

THE ROARING OF THE ENEMY

Even though God told Moses of the delays, for Israel and even Moses it looked like they would not be freed. It was the roaring of the enemy. At the first meeting of Moses and Pharaoh, it appeared that Pharaoh was too strong even for the name of God: I Am. Pharaoh burdened the people even more, forcing them to make bricks finding their own straw. Moses and Israel were dismayed as the enemy roared. *"Then Moses returned to the LORD and said, 'O Lord, why have You brought harm to this people? Why did You ever send me? Ever since I came to Pharaoh to speak in Your name, he has done harm to this people, and You have not delivered Your people at all'" (Exodus 5:22-23).* This event appeared to be harmful. However, it and the ten plagues that followed were caused by God, in order to bring about His glory both to Egypt and Israel. *"But I will harden Pharaoh's heart that I may multiply My signs and My wonders in the land of Egypt."*

Finally, the day of their freedom arrived. God was not finished with Egypt or Israel. More of His glory was yet to be revealed in the freeing of His people and the judgment of Egypt. *"But I will also judge the nation whom they will serve."* We can speculate about the hardening of Pharaoh's heart, but the reality was God had judged Pharaoh and his nation. They were under judgment and the penalty was that they, Israel's enemy, would be destroyed by the plagues and the Red Sea.

SATAN

I want to add here that Satan does not have the same abilities as God. He has no foresight. I believe, as events unfold, he is a spectator: either cheering as he sees events in his favor or going away defeated and planning a new strategy to defeat God and His beloved creation: man.

Satan did not see that God was using him in the testing of Job. Sometimes Satan thinks he causes events. After God granted Satan the right to test Job, I believe Satan thought his accusations would be proven true about God and Job.

I also believe that every time God hardened Pharaoh, Satan was delighted. Each time Pharaoh's heart was hardened, Satan, the enemy, roared. However, it was all in God's greater plan. In like manner, we are God's plan -- His purpose -- His good for His glory and our eternity. Amen!

GOD'S DELIBERATE SOVEREIGNTY
HEARTACHE AND TRAGEDY

In exploring God's deliberate sovereignty, this is how I understand God interacts with us. For instance, heartache and tragedy are a part of life. Joy and triumph are also life experiences. The reality is we live in a broken, sinful, and corrupted world full of sinful people and evil intentions. Indeed, evil is in the world. Just looking at the nightly news of beheadings, mass slayings, rape, murder, and on and on. These are all the proof needed. Sometimes heartache and tragedy come to us as a result of others' actions, and sometimes our own.

Disease and death are a part of our reality. They entered the world because of our sin. They are not God caused, but sin and rebellion caused. Sometimes our own sin unknowingly or knowingly causes heartache and tragedy. For instance, my generation did not know the deadly consequences of smoking in our own lives, our family's lives through second hand smoke, or in pregnancy. Still, look at how much heartache and tragedy smoking caused through ignorance. Even in this day, knowing about smoking's consequences, we could say indifference or open rebellious behavior causes disease and death. People smoke, despite knowing it is harmful to them and others.

It is the same with alcohol. It hurts our bodies. The effects of drunken or alcoholic parents on spouses, children, or others is tragic. If someone drives drunk and kills one of our loved ones, it is by another's action. If I drive drunk and kill myself or someone else, it is by my own action.

Mostly of my previous discussion was about God's deliberate acts in the lives and events of *"those who love God, to those who are called according to His purpose."* In the Old Testament, they were called Israelites. In the New Testament, they are called Israelites and Christians. We who know God and His calling in our lives come, hopefully, to maturity about God. We are willing to live in His purpose even through heartache and tragedy. They are painful, but most of us come to peace and hope about God's working in our lives. God works through heartache and tragedy. We, through testing, and even through fire, come to trust God. Indeed, it is because of the fiery ordeals that our trust matures.

> *"In this you greatly rejoice, even though now for a little while, if necessary, you have been distressed by various trials, so that the proof of your faith, being more precious than gold which is perishable, even though tested by fire, may be found to result in praise and glory and honor at the revelation of Jesus Christ; and though you have not seen Him, you love Him, and though you do not see Him now, but believe in Him, you greatly rejoice with joy inexpressible and full of glory, obtaining as the outcome of your faith the salvation of your souls" (1 Peter 1:6-9).*

But what about heartache and tragedy in the lives of those who do not love God or those who will not respond or have not yet responded to His call? God works through individual life events to bring about His purpose for His church and also in the individual lives of people. God is always working in the events of those who do not love Him in hopes of bringing them to repentance. *"The Lord is not slow about His promise, as some count slowness, but is patient toward you, not wishing for any to perish but for all to come to repentance" (2 Peter 3:9).* Yes, God knows if we will respond or not, but still He gives us the opportunity. Ultimately, God works through everything to His purpose, just as He worked through the persecutions of Saul against the Church. The result was the Gospel spreading throughout the region and many people coming to salvation. Also, Saul's life was saved through his persecution.

Those outside of God as well as those in Him are all part of His sovereign plan. God can work through evil people, governments, and institutions to bring about his purpose. Similarly, God used Satan to bring about His purpose. All the exorcisms in the New Testament were used to show the authority of Jesus over demons and Satan their leader. It demonstrated how much God loved to set the captives free. Satan's testing of our Lord in the desert is another example. The desert testing demonstrated Jesus was without sin, as well as the power of God's Word over sin and the tempter, Satan.

Pharaoh is another example: God hardened His heart to bring about His glory. Pharaoh lost his first born son, his wealth, and the power of his army in that exchange. However, one thing is certain: Pharaoh came to know God is real.

Trails of Punishment - Judgment

I wonder how many times our suffering or trials are set up and allowed for a divine purpose we cannot see or understand. As a matter of fact, I believe each and every trial is God-ordained and part of His divine purpose, even if the trial is punishment meant to lead us to repentance.

> *And you have forgotten the exhortation which is addressed to you as sons, "MY SON, DO NOT REGARD LIGHTLY THE DISCIPLINE OF THE LORD, NOR FAINT WHEN YOU ARE REPROVED BY HIM; FOR THOSE WHOM THE LORD LOVES HE DISCIPLINES, AND HE SCOURGES EVERY SON WHOM HE RECEIVES." It is for discipline that you endure; God deals with you as with sons; for what son is there whom his father does not discipline? (Hebrews 12:5-7)*

Yes, sometimes trial, heartache, and loss come by way of discipline. Sometimes it comes because of judgment. The story of Ananias and Sapphira is an example of the latter.

> *But there was a certain man named Ananias*
> *who, with his wife, Sapphira, sold some prop-*
> *erty. He brought part of the money to the apos-*
> *tles, claiming it was the full amount. With his*
> *wife's consent, he kept the rest. Then Peter*
> *said, "Ananias, why have you let Satan fill*
> *your heart? You lied to the Holy Spirit, and*
> *you kept some of the money for yourself. The*
> *property was yours to sell or not sell, as you*
> *wished. And after selling it, the money was*
> *also yours to give away. How could you do a*
> *thing like this? You weren't lying to us but to*
> *God!" As soon as Ananias heard these words,*
> *he fell to the floor and died. Everyone who*
> *heard about it was terrified (Acts 5:1-5).*

Thankfully, not all judgments end in death. Most judgments are meant to lead us to repentance.

> *"I now rejoice, not that you were made sor-*
> *rowful, but that you were made sorrowful to*
> *the point of repentance; for you were made*
> *sorrowful according to the will of God, so that*
> *you might not suffer loss in anything through*
> *us. For the sorrow that is according to the will*
> *of God produces a repentance without regret,*
> *leading to salvation, but the sorrow of the*
> *world produces death" (2 Corinthians 7:9-10).*

My salvation came by way of both judgment and punishment. It was when I could no longer endure a life of rebellion and its consequences that I came to my knees with pleas for mercy and forgiveness. Thank you, Lord, that you did not let me go, but caused me such sorrow in my rebellious life that it resulted in my asking for mercy and forgiveness.

As time passes, I gain understanding of previous trials, especially as lessons learned are applied to future events. I have often been thankful here in the Philippines for previous lessons that confirmed my faith and made me strong and unwavering. The trials of testing are not easy to endure. Sometimes testing causes my knees to shake. However, I thank God that He makes me strong, through trials, to lead in the mission field.

MORE ABOUT A CORRUPT AND DYING WORLD

"For the creation was subjected to futility, not willingly, but because of Him who subjected it, in hope that the creation itself also will be set free from its slavery to corruption into the freedom of the glory of the children of God" (Romans 8:20-21).

The result of Adam's and Eve's sin, as well as ours, was death entering into the world. God pronounced the judgment and penalty.

To the woman He said, *"I will greatly multiply Your pain in childbirth, In pain you will
bring forth children; Yet your desire will be
for your husband, And he will rule over you.
Then to Adam He said, "Because you have listened to the voice of your wife, and have eaten
from the tree about which I commanded you,
saying, 'You shall not eat from it'; Cursed is
the ground because of you; In toil you will eat
of it All the days of your life. "Both thorns and
thistles it shall grow for you; And you will eat
the plants of the field; By the sweat of your
face You will eat bread, Till you return to the
ground, Because from it you were taken; For
you are dust, And to dust you shall return.
(Genesis 3:16-19)*

Those who don't know God want to blame Him for
death, disease, and injustice in the world. And these
things do exist. We all get sick and die. We have all felt
the pain of injustice in our lives. It is part of the cursed
world we live in.

We brought this about through disobedience. None of
us can stand before God and say we are undeserving of
the consequence of sin. *"Therefore, just as through one
man sin entered into the world, and death through sin, and
so death spread to all men, because all sinned" (Romans
5:12).* I often humorously say when teaching this truth, "If
you are without sin, raise your hand."

We see the same reaction in our children when we enact judgment and punishment to them. I can remember when I was younger, going to my room for a punishment, thinking how unfair and unjust my mother was. However, as she pronounced the punishment, she would always say, "You can come out of your room when you realize why I sent you there and you apologize for your behavior." It is the same with our Lord. When we come to realize our plight of sin and its consequences and come to repentance, we are forgiven: our lives restored.

There is injustice in the world because of evil men and their institutions, governments, and religions. Also, I've seen, most regrettably, evil from false judgment, hypocrisy and legalism in so-called Christian churches. However, God works through these also, just as He did through Pharaoh of Egypt.

GOD IS PERSONAL

Finally, as I come to know Him -- as we work together -- I come to know our relationship is secure and dependable. I trust Him. Therefore, everything that happens to me, whether pain or joy, is acceptable to me.

In the working of His will is also my personal relationship with Him. God answers my prayers. He knows my tears. The Holy Spirit searches my heart. From my mother's womb, He knit me together. He knew my name before the foundations of the world. He allows me, by grace and mercy, the privilege of working in His will to accomplish His will in my life and others'. He has ordained me a servant to accomplish the task He has set before me (Ref: John 1:12; Hebrews 4:16; 4:13; Psalm 56:8; Romans 8:26-27; Psalm 139:13; Revelation 13:8; Ephesians 3:7-8). *"Be on guard for yourselves and for all the flock, among* <u>*which the Holy Spirit has made you overseers,*</u> *to shepherd the church of God which He purchased with His own blood"* *(Acts 20:28).*

Our prayers and intimate relationship with God can shape things. They too are a part of God's sovereign plan, known from before creation.

Abraham bargaining with God over the judgement and destruction of Sodom is a good example. Abraham bargained God all the way down to just ten found righteous to save the city. *"'Only this once; suppose ten are found there?' And He said, 'I will not destroy it on account of the ten'"* *(Genesis 18:32).*

I believe God knew Abraham's heart and allowed him to partner with Him in judgment and salvation. It was the same with God knowing Satan would accuse both Himself and Job. God knew Job would be faithful. God knew the compassion of Abraham's heart. God works His purpose though everything.

God hears and answers our prayers for our own lives, and those we love or are called to shepherd. *"For we do not have a high priest who cannot sympathize with our weaknesses, but One who has been tempted in all things as we are, yet without sin. Therefore let us draw near with confidence to the throne of grace, so that we may receive mercy and find grace to help in time of need"* *(Hebrews 4:15, 16).*

I love my deliberate God
I Love this deliberate life He gave me
I love His deliberate love for me
He is sovereign and I trust Him

In Closing, Consider Hannah

Hannah's God, our God, is personal and sovereign. She prayed for our Lord to give her a son. She knew the sovereignty of our Lord. She knew her womb was shut by the Lord and only He could open it. She prayed for a son, combining her prayer with a vow to God.

> *"She made a vow and said, 'O LORD of hosts, if You will indeed look on the affliction of Your maidservant and remember me, and not forget Your maidservant, but will give Your maidservant a son, then I will give him to the LORD all the days of his life, and a razor shall never come on his head'" (1 Samuel 1:11).*

The Lord answered her prayer and gave her a son. After she weaned him, she fulfilled her vow. Here is her prayer.

> *"Then Hannah prayed and said, 'My heart exults in the LORD; My horn is exalted in the LORD, My mouth speaks boldly against my enemies, Because I rejoice in Your salvation.' There is no one holy like the LORD, Indeed, there is no one*

besides You, Nor is there any rock like our God. Boast no more so very proudly, Do not let arrogance come out of your mouth; For the LORD is a God of knowledge, And with Him actions are weighed. The bows of the mighty are shattered, But the feeble gird on strength. Those who were full hire themselves out for bread, But those who were hungry cease to hunger. Even the barren gives birth to seven, But she who has many children languishes. The LORD kills and makes alive; He brings down to Sheol and raises up. The LORD makes poor and rich; He brings low, He also exalts. He raises the poor from the dust, He lifts the needy from the ash heap To make them sit with nobles, And inherit a seat of honor; For the pillars of the earth are the LORD'S, And He set the world on them" (1 Samuel 2:1-8).

I pray what I have come to know about God will inspire you as it does me. I pray it will give you peace and confidence as you face life with God.

"O LORD, You are my God; I will exalt You, I will give thanks to Your name; For You have worked wonders, Plans formed long ago, with perfect faithfulness" (Isaiah 25:1).

PLEASE COME BACK

Pastor Alejo F. Alagos – The Denomination –
Tabernacle of Praise Christian Center – Franks/Mabasa
Church – Mount Horeb Church

"But as for me and my house, we will serve the
LORD" (Joshua 24:15b ESV).

AS I MENTIONED BEFORE, PASTOR ALAGOS WAS ONE
of the men who gathered the Grace Chapel congregation
for the dedication. Both he and Brother Jojo continued
to hold regular services at Grace Chapel. It was at the
dedication that I met Pastor Alagos for the first time. We
became instant friends.

PASTOR ALAGOS

At that time, Pastor Alagos was the Assistant
Superintendent of Antique Province for his denomination. (I will not mention the denomination name because
we have had many problems with and persecutions from

them. As this chapter unfolds, you will understand why I choose not to name them).

Pastor Alagos was nominated to be the Superintendent for the Province of Antique for this denomination. In his first twenty-five years of ministry, he had planted twenty-five churches. He is also an elementary school principal for several schools, and teaches masters level courses in education at one of the colleges.

THE DENOMINATION

It was during the time of my arrival that Pastor Alagos was having a difficult time with his denomination. Because positions in the denomination were by vote, the process became very political. As with other political organizations, jealousies arose and dirty politics became the norm to acquire power, prestige, and money in the race to the top. Pastor Alagos wanted nothing to do with this, but he was nominated and was having trouble pulling his name from the nomination. He was held in high esteem by most for his wisdom and ability to start new churches.

We had already started three churches together while I was in America. I raised funds and he, with his team's help, supervised the church launches. We worked well as partners in this ministry.

During this time, he was wrestling with continuing in the denomination. I told him that I had no denomination. I worked for the Lord and was accountable only to Jesus and the elders of my home church in the USA. I am a pastor in God's Church: the church described in the New Testament. *"I am writing to God's church in Corinth, to you who have been called by God to be His own holy people. He made you holy by means of Christ Jesus, just as He did for all people everywhere who call on the name of our Lord Jesus Christ, their Lord and ours" (1 Corinthians 1:2 NLT).*

The elders of my sending church in America are godly men that met the Biblical qualifications of elders and spiritual leadership. I submit to them as the Lord would have me do. Humility and accountability are godly principles.

However, the denomination Pastor Alagos was involved with had slipped away from God's Church. They were now men of self-importance, as was their denomination. *"For many walk, of whom I often told you, and now tell you even weeping, that they are enemies of the cross of Christ, whose end is destruction, whose god is their appetite, and whose glory is in their shame, who set their minds on earthly things" (Philippians 3:18, 19).*

Pastor Alagos finally submitted his resignation from the denomination. After many meetings, they reluctantly accepted it. Pastor Alagos continued to pastor one of our churches, Tabernacle of Praise Christian Center (TOP).

I remember well the day Pastor Alagos told me about his resignation. He said, "Now I work only for the Lord." What a huge release it was for him. Jesus said all authority has been given to Him. Now therefore go into all the world!

"And Jesus came up and spoke to them, saying, 'All authority has been given to Me in heaven

> *and on earth* <u>*Go therefore*</u> *and make disci-*
> *ples of all the nations, baptizing them in the*
> *name of the Father and the Son and the Holy*
> *Spirit, teaching them to observe all that I com-*
> *manded you; and lo<u>, I am with you always,*</u>
> *even to the end of the age'" (Matthew 28:18-20).*

In whose authority do we go? Jesus'! Why do we go?
Because Jesus sends us. What do we do? Teach about
Jesus, baptize in the name of the Father, Son, and Holy
Spirit, and teach them to do the same. It is all and only
about Jesus. It is never about churches, denominations,
or us. It is never about title, position, prestige, power,
or wealth. It is only about Jesus' authority and name,
and proclaiming His message. That is why we go! That is
what we do!

> *"Being found in appearance as a man, He hum-*
> *bled Himself by becoming obedient to the point*
> *of death, even death on a cross. For this reason*
> *also, <u>God highly exalted Him,</u> and <u>bestowed on*</u>
> <u>*Him the name which is above every name,*</u> *so*
> *that <u>at the name of Jesus EVERY KNEE WILL*</u>
> <u>*BOW,*</u> *of those who are in heaven and on earth*
> *and under the earth, and that <u>every tongue*</u>
> <u>*will confess that Jesus Christ is Lord,*</u> *<u>to the*</u>
> <u>*glory of God the Father"*</u> *(Philippians 2:8-11).*

It is because of Jesus' love for us on the cross that he has been given all authority. His name is above all names and only He is Lord! Salvation is by no other name. *"And there is salvation in no one else; for there is no other name under heaven that has been given among men by which we must be saved"* *(Acts 4:12)*.

We serve no one but Jesus; we serve only in His name; only by His authority. It is Jesus Christ's Church: not ours. He purchased His Church with His blood: not ours. *"Be on guard for yourselves and for all the flock, among which the Holy Spirit has made you overseers, to shepherd the church of God which He purchased with His own blood"* *(Acts 20:28)*.

**It is when we serve ourselves,
our denomination,
our church by our power and authority,
another's power and authority,
or an organization's power and authority
that we no longer serve God.**

The roaring of the enemy was the denomination's dirty tricks of slander and lying to disqualify Pastor Alagos. It was also the question of his ordination through the denomination. He would lose his ordination. Included in his thoughts were in what or whose authority could he pastor a church? Where would his ordination come from?

THE LORD IS BLESSING

The Lord was blessing in that He was moving an honest, humble, and hardworking servant out of a denomination that was no longer serving Him. The Lord gifted Pastor Alagos and it was time he used those gifts in the Lord's Church. Pastor Alagos discovered the real Church of God. *"This letter is from Paul, chosen by the will of God to be an apostle of Christ Jesus, and from our brother Timothy. I am writing to <u>God's church in Corinth and to all of His holy people throughout Greece</u>" (2 Corinthians 1:1).*

God's universal church was purchased by the blood of Jesus Christ and has existed since the day of Pentecost. It is not a denomination, but His church: made up everyone who has called upon Jesus' name. *"All who in every place call on the name of our Lord Jesus Christ, their Lord and ours" (1 Corinthians 1:2b).*

After RRCP registered with the Security and Exchange Commission (SEC) of the Philippines, the elders of our home church decided unanimously to appoint and ordain Alejo Alagos as a pastor for RRCP. RRCP is simply a part of God's Church serving in the Philippines. We are currently thirty churches serving as God's Church throughout the Philippines, primarily in the isolated remote areas. We serve under the shepherding of our home church in America and the appointed elders of RRCP locally. Our supporters are worldwide, including many churches and denominations.

TABERNACLE OF PRAISE CHRISTIAN CENTER (TOP)

TOP was our second church. When I was in the Philippines the first time in 2006 for the dedication of Grace Chapel, Pastor Alagos told me he had a radio ministry that had become popular. However, he needed sponsors to continue. So we decided to support the radio ministry.

THE BIRTH OF TOP

The radio ministry had many requests for live broadcasts from listener barangays. In 2007, one of the live broadcast was from Barangay (community) Mabasa, Patnongon, Antique. Several people were led to the Lord on that live broadcast, including the barangay captain and a retired chemical engineer: Alejandro (Alex) D. Dongon. Later, he became our first RRCP elder in 2015. In 2016 he was ordained as pastor of RRCP. Pastor Alex is close to getting a BA in theology. He pastors our Mount Horeb Church in Magarang, Patnongon, Antique as well.

In 2007, the Ungsod family of Mabasa, TOP church members, offered a portion of land near their home to build a bamboo church building. There the church grew.

They began praying for land near the main road so they could build a larger concrete block and plaster church building. Another member of the church offered a nice piece of land on the main road. She and her family also donated most of the money to build the church building.

Others of the congregation, including Pastor Alagos, made substantial donations as well. The donor of the land promised to deed the land and church building to TOP once it was finished, including a parsonage next to the church for the Alagos family.

THE ENEMY ROARED

After Pastor Alagos resigned from the denomination, they decided they wanted the new TOP church building and land. Leaders of the denomination convinced the owner of the land that if she gave the building and land to the denomination, they would post her nephew as the pastor. As a result, the owner started placing unrealistic demands on the TOP congregation that could not be met. The leaders of the denomination also went door to door in Mabasa, telling the community that Pastor Alagos and I like to drink and get drunk. They said Pastor Alagos was asked to leave the denomination due to character issues. They went to the superintendent of schools and accused Principal Alagos of misappropriating school funds. I think the euphemism for this is "Political Dirty Tricks."

THE LORD IS BLESSING – PLEASE COME BACK

The elders and leaders of the TOP congregation had a meeting and decided to leave the church building. They rented a venue bordering the Mabasa and Igbarawan barangays. As they left the building, they ceremoniously wiped the dust off their feet, just as Jesus told the seventy disciples He sent out to bless the cities with the message of the Kingdom to do. *"But whatever city you enter and they do not receive you, go out into its streets and say, 'Even the dust of your city which clings to our feet we wipe off in protest against you; yet be sure of this, that the kingdom of God has come near'" (Luke 10:10, 11).*

The next day, the denomination changed the name on the church building. As promised, they appointed the new pastor. They wanted the beautiful church building and they got it. To this day, with the exception of special denomination events, it sits empty. The church is not a building, but all who call upon the name of the Lord in every time and place. God's Church is the people of God.

The next Sunday at the rented venue, the TOP congregation doubled. It now drew people from both barangays. In the meantime, the Mabasa barangay council lamented losing Pastor Alagos. For more than two years, he went to pray with anyone who was sick and meet with families in distress. The church showed up at every passing of a family member in the community. Pastor Alagos and the TOP congregation loved the Mabasa people whether or not they had a church background. The Mabasa community had lost their pastor.

The Mabasa council approached Pastor Alagos and said that if he were to move the TOP church back to Mabasa, they would find land for him to construct a church building. However, the church decided not to move back, because TOP in the new venue was reaching a lot of people and growing. So they built a new church building in the Franks area of Mabasa for a new congregation. It is called the Franks/Mabasa Church. Franks is a squatter's area where the poorest of the poor live. I always feel the presence of the Lord there.

> *"'For I was hungry, and you gave Me something to eat; I was thirsty, and you gave Me something to drink; I was a stranger, and you invited Me in; naked, and you clothed Me; I was sick, and you visited Me; I was in prison, and you came to Me.' "Then the righteous will answer Him, 'Lord, when did we see You hungry, and feed You, or thirsty, and give You something to drink? 'And when did we see You a stranger, and invite You in, or naked, and clothe You? 'When did we see You sick, or in prison, and come to You?' "The King will answer and say to them, 'Truly I say to you, to the extent that you did it to one of these brothers of Mine, even the least of them, you did it to Me'"* (Matthew 25:35-40).

Franks/Mabasa serves *"the least of them"* for sure. That is why I feel the presence of the Lord there. Shortly after the Franks/Mabasa church was built, Super Typhoon Yolanda hit the Philippines. The eye of the typhoon was just above our island. After the typhoon, we fed Franks and

Mabasa people nearly 2000 pounds of rice and repaired more than a dozen homes.

A year later the new mosquito-borne disease Chikungunya hit the Philippines. It is debilitating and can be deadly. Mabasa was the epicenter. We went door to door surveying who was sick and then supplied the medications necessary.

THE BLESSINGS CONTINUED

In addition, the superintendent of schools did an investigation into the allegations presented by the denomination. Principal Alejo Alagos was found innocent. In fact, as a result of the investigation, Principal Alagos received awards for outstanding performance as an elementary school principal. I believe that had the superintendent not investigated Principal Alagos, these accomplishments would have gone unnoticed.

Soon after, Principal Alagos was moved to Igbarawan Elementary School near his home. Before, he had traveled a great distance to and from work. The new school made his life easier and gave him more time to serve the Lord.

CHILDREN'S CARE CENTER (CCC)

The students of his new elementary school are from Franks, Mabasa and Igbarawan. He now not only pastored the community but also educated the children. Once there, he identified sixty-five severely malnourished children who were seriously behind in school. He developed the Children's Care Center (CCC), run out of the Franks/ Mabasa church building. This was a weekend program that tutored the kids back to grade level. It also fed the children four nutritious meals on the weekend to bring them out of malnourishment. In addition, their parents were taught family hygiene and how to help their children through school. After one year, they all graduated. Many are entering high school now. The CCC program was funded through RRCP supporters. We now have a new batch of children in the program.

MORE BLESSINGS – MORE CHURCHES

Shortly after the persecution and moving to the new venue, another member of TOP offered land in Barangay Magarang, Patnongon, Antique. There we established another church called Mount Horeb Church. The once persecuted church is now three churches. GOD IS GOOD – THANK YOU, LORD.

A PERMANENT HOME

The TOP congregation had moved many times: from a bamboo Mabasa home church to the Mabasa main road, and then the new venue between Mabasa and Igbarawan. It was truly a tabernacle: a moving tabernacle of our Lord. The congregation was praying for a permanent home.

Also without a parsonage, the Alagos family was living on the floor of their small bakery at night. The heat of the

Philippines plus the added heat of the bakery oven made the living conditions almost unbearable. Pastor Alagos, Edna and their four teen children lived in a 10x10 foot area, sleeping on the floor and on tables. The blessing came a year later, when we attached to the Franks/Mabasa church a large parsonage for them to live in.

Finally, a donation came to build a new TOP church. The congregation purchased a lot and we built the new church home. Like in the book of Acts, persecution led to a growing church.

The denomination has since split. They are suing each other in court, and under investigation for misappropriated funds. Two of the leaders responsible for the persecution of TOP and Pastor Alagos became seriously sick. Could it be God's judgement?

They have not stopped their persecution. It continues to this day with our churches on the island of Palawan. Each time they pursue us they are embarrassed publicly, our congregations grow stronger, and our pastors become more united in our effort to establish more churches. One of the denomination's national superintendents publicly declared they would take over all of our churches. This is amazing to me. The harvest is upon us. Let us stop wasting energy and resources and enter the harvest. We have learned to ignore them except when it is impossible.

> *"Jesus was going through all the cities and villages, teaching in their synagogues and proclaiming the gospel of the kingdom, and*

healing every kind of disease and every kind of sickness. Seeing the people, He felt compassion for them, because they were distressed and dispirited like sheep without a shepherd. Then He said to His disciples, "The harvest is plentiful, but the workers are few. Therefore beseech the Lord of the harvest to send out workers into His harvest" (Matthew 9:35-38).

Pastor Alejo Alagos

Tabernacle of Praise Christian Center

Franks/Mabasa & CCC

Mount Horeb Church

THEY STOOD BESIDE THEIR PASTOR

Pastor Stephen and Sarah Mahusay – The Island Palawan - The Denomination

"I've commanded you, haven't I? Be strong and courageous. Don't be fearful or discouraged, because the LORD your God is with you wherever you go" (Joshua 1:9).

IN 2012, ONE YEAR AFTER WE ARRIVED, WE WANTED TO take Pastor Alagos and Edna to America to meet the home church there. The US Embassy denied them a visa. It is typical, as only one in fifty Filipinos are granted visas to the US. However, my family and I went on to America without Pastor Alagos and Edna to give a report to the church.

In the meantime, Pastor Alagos' niece Sarah and her husband Stephen Mahusay had a Bible study going in Barangay Santa Lourdes, Puerto Princesa, on the island of Palawan. Up to this point, all of our churches were on the island of Panay, where Pastor Alagos and I live.

Pastor Stephen and Sarah met while attending a two-year Bible school. There they fell in love and were married. They were also a part of the denomination Pastor Alagos was in previously. The denomination had revoked Pastor Stephen and Sarah's preaching license from them three years earlier. The denomination had deemed them illiterate: interesting, since they graduated from a two-year Bible school.

Pastor Stephen and Sarah continued serving the Lord and started an independent Bible study. Much counseling from Pastor Alagos was required for Stephen and Sarah during this time. They are far from illiterate and their hearts were crushed.

Pastor Alagos had arranged a two-week vacation from the Department of Education, anticipating visiting the USA. Now with no visa and two weeks free, Pastor Alagos and Edna went to Palawan to launch our first church there at Barangay Santa Lourdes. Pastor Stephen, Sarah, and their Bible study helped launch the church. It was a wonderful success. We launched with a two-night Concert Crusade. Many came to the Lord and later would become church leaders.

The Santa Lourdes House Church grew. About one year later, we were able to build a church building for them. The land was donated by one of the members, and RRCP provided the funds to construct the building. Everything was registered into the legal entity of RRCP.

THE ENEMY ROARING

Before the paint was dry, the denomination showed up, claiming the building and property belong to them. They came with an attorney and a surveyor. They surveyed the property and handed Pastor Stephen and Sarah a written notice that they would post one of their own pastors to the church. Pastor Stephen and Sarah called Pastor Alagos in a panic and we were soon on a plane to Palawan.

Once there, the secretary of the denomination met with Pastor Stephen, Sarah, Pastor Alagos, and me. Sarah's father was also there. He had once been a pastor for the denomination as well. They had asked him to leave the denomination a few years earlier because he was planting churches in remote areas and the denomination only wanted to plant churches in the cities.

We explained that the church was owned legally by RRCP and they had no claim to the land and building. However, the denomination secretary insisted they did have a right because Pastor Stephen and Sarah, even though they were inactive and their licenses had been revoked for the last three years, were still considered a part of the domination. The denomination has a clause in their bylaws that states that if one of the pastors starts a church, the property and building belong to the denomination, regardless of who actually owns the land and the building. The secretary was claiming even inactive pastors and those who have left the denomination fall under this rule. We told the secretary that if necessary we would let a judge determine the matter.

After the meeting, we went back home to Panay. Not long after, the denomination showed up with one of their pastors on a Sunday morning. They wanted to post their pastor to the church officially. The congregation refused to allow the denomination pastor to enter.

The next week, Pastor Alagon went to Palawan and met with our attorney. She examined the letter stating they would post their pastor and that the land and building belonged to the denomination. The letter was signed by their attorney. Our attorney investigated their attorney and discovered he was a fraud, as was the surveyor and his survey. She quickly fired off a letter to them and told them she would see them in jail for misrepresenting an officer of the court and falsifying land documents. For a long time they became silent and this round was closed.

Later we learned that years earlier the denomination had their claim tested in court. This was a bigger church that could afford to fight the denomination legally. The church won that decision. Even though the denomination lost the one case, they continue to use the same tactic on smaller churches that are less sophisticated and don't know they have rights. The denomination takes over many properties and church buildings this way. In the process, they are accumulating wealth with land and buildings.

The roaring of the enemy was the denomination threatening the congregation and RRCP that they owned the building and Stephen and Sarah would no longer be their pastor. It was indeed an attempt at a classic hostile takeover.

THE LORD IS BLESSING

Pastor Stephen and Sarah became strong as they stood against the enemy and protected their flock from a godless organization. Indeed, our Lord was with them. The congregation stood beside their pastor. In doing so, they healed the hearts of Stephen and Sarah. The church became united and strong. Remarkably, many pastors, leaders, and elders would come from this church. They all witnessed the power and providence of God as He led them to victory against a cunning adversary. As of today, the Santa Lourdes church has planted fourteen more churches on the island of Palawan. More churches are being started as I write this.

I think it an interesting note that this alleged "illiterate couple" is responsible for fourteen new churches in Palawan within three years. It is not because of their unique ability but because of their unique faith. *"But God has chosen the foolish things of the world to shame the wise, and God has chosen the weak things of the world to shame the things which are strong" (1 Corinthians 1:27).*

ANOTHER BLESSING

Elder Tito and wife Telde Fidel were the original house church for Santa Lourdes. At that time, they were having trouble selling their home and land. It had been for sale two years. They asked Pastor Alagos and me to pray for the sale of their home and we did. Just a few months later, the home sold for a very good price. They tithed the sale to the church. The large sum of money paid for Pastor Stephen's motorcycle (motorcycles are a primary mode of transportation), sound equipment for the church, and many other blessings.

Brother Tito purchased a large piece of property for their new home near Pastor Stephen's home in Barangay Maranat. They started a new Bible study there and it later became our Maranat Riverside Church. Just this last year, Tito became our first elder for Palawan. He stood strong against the denomination and loves Stephen and Sarah. Both their homes became house churches that out-grew their homes and now have church buildings. Both churches are vibrant and growing.

> *"My eyes shall be upon the faithful of the land, that they may dwell with me; He who walks in a blameless way is the one who will min-ister to me.*
>
> *He who practices deceit shall not dwell within my house; He who speaks falsehood shall not maintain his position before me" (Psalm 101:6, 7).*

Pastor Stephen and Sarah Mahusay

RRCP Santa Lourdes Our First Church at Palawan

PERSECUTION TO BLESSING

*Barangay Tagumpay - Pastor Larry and Judy –
Barangay Candaleria*

*"Therefore, since we have a great high priest
who has gone to heaven, Jesus the Son of God,
let us live our lives consistent with our confession
of faith.*

*For we do not have a high priest who is unable
to sympathize with our weaknesses. Instead,
we have one who in every respect has been
tempted as we are, yet he never sinned.*

*So let us keep on coming boldly to the throne
of grace, so that we may obtain mercy and
find grace to help us in our time of need"
(Hebrews 4:14-16).*

BARANGAY TAGUMPAY

NOT LONG AFTER THE SANTA LOURDES CHURCH WAS saved from the denomination, we decided to plant another church in Barangay Tagumpay, Roxas Palawan. Pastor Alagos and Sarah had family there: Christians with no place to congregate and worship. Tagumpay is nearly three hours of travel one way by motorcycle from Santa Lourdes. We arranged a church launch with a two-night Christian Concert Crusade. Pastor Alagos and I traveled to Palawan to participate in the crusade. We had also arranged a pastor for the congregation. Pastor Alagos, Stephen, and Sarah knew him.

We rented two vans to haul the sound equipment, Pastor Alagos, leaders of the Santa Lourdes Church, and me. In addition, there were six motorcycles full of people.

In the Philippines, you will sometimes see as many as seven on one motorcycle. In America, we have the family car. In the Philippines, for many, it is the family motorcycle. However, the convoy was only two to three people per motorcycle.

We arrived a day early and went house to house inviting the barangay. As usual, we obtained a permit from the Barangay captain. He and members of the council were in attendance for the launch. Our reputation of helping people with feeding programs, Operation Kindness, and other care ministries had preceded us. The Barangay council received us with open arms.

Each night, more than 150 people showed up for the crusade. The Spirit of God was moving and about thirty people came forward and gave their hearts to the Lord. Many people also recommitted their lives to God. The second night had the same results. Three Bible studies were started, which later became *Christ's Church Transformation Center RRCP*.

Tagumpay in particular is extremely poor. The barangay floods every year during typhoon season -- sometimes as much as eight feet deep. The houses are built off the ground: bamboo houses with bamboo poles holding them up. Because of flooding, it is nearly impossible to plant crops or raise animals like chickens, goats, and pigs.

I am happy to report that, since we established the church there three years ago, no flooding has occurred. The barangay is improving in health and quality of life. This is the case every time we enter a new barangay. When people come to know the Lord and their sins are forgiven, it opens the door for answered prayers and blessings from our Lord. It is also my observation that once the church is established, worship to our Lord becomes consistent, and people begin to forgive and love one another, blessings flow on the entire community.

Jesus said, *"You have heard that it was said, 'You must love your neighbor' and hate your enemy. But I say to you, love your enemies, and pray for those who persecute you, so that you will become children of your Father in heaven, because he makes his sun rise on both evil and good people,*

and he lets rain fall on the righteous and the unrighteous"
(Matthew 5:43-45 ISV).

Before the new pastor arrived, the pastor's wife became sick. Even though they wanted to move to Tagumpay, it was not good for her health. Therefore, the pastor decided not to take the church for the sake of his family. Now the church was to be ministered to by the pastors and leaders of the Santa Lourdes church. They traveled weekly, three hours each way, for visitation and to hold a worship service in the house churches that had been created. It was a three-motorcycle convoy of Brother Tito and wife Telde, Pastor Stephen and Sarah, and Pastor Purdencio and wife Nena.

They traveled and held the worship service on Saturday. They returned Saturday evening so they would be home in time for services at their own churches Sunday morning. It took more than a year to find a pastor for the Tagumpay church.

PASTOR LARRY AND JUDY

Meanwhile, Pastor Alagos was counseling Pastor Larry and Judy, who pastored a big church in San Jose near where we live. They were respected and had a good salary (a salary for a pastor is unusual here). Many professionals attended this church.

Unfortunately, Larry discovered he had diabetes. The doctors had trouble getting his medication adjusted and Larry was having trouble dedicating time to ministering.

The church was coveted by the denomination. While Larry was sick, their pastors moved in, convincing the church leaders to let Larry and Judy go. One of the denomination's pastors took over the church. Larry and Judy's reputation was assaulted and ruined. The whole affair was quite brutal and nasty, much like they tried to do with Pastor Alagos. Their tactics are to attack character, even with lies.

Pastor Larry and Judy were devastated: both became depressed. They visited Pastor Alagos for counseling for about a year. He was able to help and restore them. During this time, they started another church and it was beginning to grow. The denomination soon wanted the new church as well.

Pastor Alagos learned that Pastor Larry and Judy once pastored a church in Palawan and were praying to return. We had a church that needed a pastor in Palawan. God is so awesome! He is in complete control.

We had not yet built the church building in Tagumpay. Pastor Larry and Judy were excited and went ahead. One of the church members let them live in an 8x8 foot bamboo room. They lived there almost a year.

Soon, they secured land for us to purchase and the church building construction started. We discovered too late that a culvert used for drainage was old and weak. Therefore, the land where we built the church was not accessible by delivery truck, so the cost of human labor to haul supplies including sand for the cement put us at an overrun in labor cost. To this day, the floor is dirt, even for the parsonage. Lord willing, this year we will complete the construction of both the church and parsonage.

BARANGAY CANDALERIA

Pastor Larry and Judy are serious about evangelism. Almost immediately after their arrival, they made contact in Barangay Candaleria. Candaleria is nine kilometers from Tagumpay. It is only accessible by dirt road. In the rainy season, it is slick mud all the way. At that time, Pastor Larry and Judy walked in and sometimes caught rides on caribou sleds or motorcycles going that way. Thank you Lord, that about a year later we were able to buy them a motorcycle. Since then they have three house churches and several Bible studies going.

Candaleria could be considered the poorest area we serve. All the communities we serve are very poor but this one is severe. It is a small isolated mountain community. There are only about 25 families. Out of these families, we identified sixty-nine moderate to severe malnourished children.

We started a weekly feeding program that helped. Later the Candaleria and Tagumpay Barangays started contributing some food as well. Judy discovered the parents were only feeding the children once a day. She started teaching about nourishment and hygiene. This was indeed a big part of the children coming out of malnourishment.

Today, almost three years later, all of the children are doing well. The effects of malnourishment still exist, but the children are doing much better. Even the parents are cleaner and healthier. When we visit now, the children are clean, dressed in clean clothes, full of energy, and happy. The Palawan government has decide to put a connecting road through Candaleria. As a result, they have provided money to rebuild the water storage tank, making the water cleaner. They have also rebuilt the elementary school. God is blessing the people of the barangay. God's church is established there, people are being saved, our Lord Jesus is worshiped, and our Lord is answering prayers and blessing the community.

A PRAISE FOR PASTORA JUDY

Judy has no children of her own. She and all of us acknowledge she has hundreds of children. Truly, she ministers to them all like her own. One of the Candaleria children, severely malnourished, was unusually small and had a hearing problem. She was constantly digging in her ear with her finger. Because of poor hygiene, wax and dirt had built up in both ears. We sent her to the doctor to look at her ears. It took several cleanings before her ears were clean. She can hear just a little now. Judy has taken a lot of time and patience to teach the girl to speak. Her first word was Jesus.

Pastor Larry and Judy have found a resource to help their churches with hygiene education, family planning (not like America's family planning – there is no abortion in the Philippines), and livelihood projects. The communities, and their leaders, love Pastor Larry and Judy.

THE ROARING OF THE ENEMY

The enemy roared when our first pastor and family could not serve, leaving a new church without a pastor. He roared in the lives of Pastor Larry and Judy when the denomination took their church. He roared again when the denomination followed them to a new church.

The enemy roared when the pastors traveled great distances weekly to serve the Tagumpay church. He roared against them with fatigue and health problems. The enemy roared at Candaleria to destroy the children and the families.

THE LORD IS BLESSING

The Lord blessed Tagumpay with a church and community who know and serve the Lord. He blessed the Santa Lourdes pastors and leaders who traveled with encounters that led to stories and praises of victory in our Lord. The Lord established resolve in their hearts, as they did not give up serving Him and His sheep in Tagumpay. He blessed Pastor Larry and Judy with communities to serve and love, unhindered by the denomination's persecution. He blessed the communities with pastors that love and serve them.

The Lord blessed Candaleria the same way. He blessed them by moving a government to come to their aid with clean water, a good school, and a road. God blessed them by moving another agency to provide hygiene and health care training, more nutritious food, and livelihood assistance.

PLEASE PRAY FOR THEM

Pastor Larry and Judy serve our Lord at a great sacrifice. There is no alternative work for them to make an extra income. They live off the small allowance RRCP is able to provide. I believe they need to fast to make ends meet -- maybe more often than I am aware. Yet they serve the Lord with excitement and great expectation from Him. They are a huge inspiration for me. Like the love of Jesus, they have no regard for themselves. They are wholly dedication to seeking the lost and ministering to our Lord's people: His sheep.

> *"Pray in the Spirit at all times and on every occasion. Stay alert and be persistent in your prayers for all believers everywhere.*
>
> *And pray for me, too. Ask God to give me the right words so I can boldly explain God's mysterious plan that the Good News is for Jews and Gentiles alike"* (Ephesians 6:18, 19).

POSTSCRIPT
THE ENEMY IS ROARING

In the last year, there have been some unfortunate events in the lives of Pastor Larry and Judy and RRCP. Things turned dramatically from blessing and praise to outburst of anger, faction, and division. Larry and Judy have now left the church. In fact, we as a church had to exercise church discipline on them.

I don't share this part of the story to condemn or embarrass them. I share it to give an assessment of the battle before us both in establishing churches and in the lives of those who serve the Lord. *"Stay alert! Watch out for your great enemy, the devil. He prowls around like a roaring lion, looking for someone to devour" (1Peter 5:8 NLT).*

Somehow, Larry and Judy were in contact with the denomination that persecuted them and RRCP. A dialogue started to reestablish their relationship.

Unknown to RRCP, the denomination began to help Larry and Judy with the ministry in Tagumpay. This same denomination proclaimed at one of their national meetings that they would take over all the RRCP churches. Larry and Judy were ministering to three RRCP churches.

The RRCP pastors and leaders in Palawan are an especially tight group that meet and co-minister on a regular basis. Up until recently, Larry and Judy were active participants and effective encouragers in the group.

Larry and Judy began missing meetings and group functions. When they did show up, they were very critical of RRCP's organizational structure. In one meeting, they brought two strangers with them and took over the meeting, angrily demanding that Palawan separate from RRCP and elect their own president, vice president, and treasurer. They demanded their treasurer be in charge of the RRCP donations for that island's churches.

OUR SOLUTIONS

In the beginning, Pastor Alagos and I made a special trip to Palawan to answer Larry and Judy's questions about how our leadership works. They seems okay with the answers and we all prayed together for forgiveness and Christian fellowship. Before this started, RRCP had recently purchased a motorcycle for them and increased their allowance. They were certainly able to attend the meetings. Now we pledged to increase their gas allowance so they could travel to the meetings as they had further to travel than the others.

They did not come to any of the meetings after that except a few, when they complained and disrupted. Pastor Alagos was in continuous contact with the Palawan leadership. He shared everything with me. I wanted to know how seriously their disruptions were affecting the Palawan church leadership. I suggested the pastors have a meeting and vote as to whether we should ask Larry and Judy to leave RRCP. The vote was 18 to 0 to have them leave. The continuous yelling, screaming, and complaints from Larry and Judy had taken their toll.

Pastor Alagos and I, along with our attorney, drafted a dis-fellowship letter and eviction notice for Larry and Judy. We were very uncomfortable through this entire process. Pastor Alagos and I decided to meet with them again before we dis-fellowshipped them. We were praying our Lord could heal and reunite us.

We flew again to Palawan to meet with Larry and Judy. We were to have a meeting with the pastors and leaders after we met with them. We had a two-hour meeting with Larry and Judy. They repented of their actions and we gave further explanation of RRCP and its government. We told them they do not have to agree with us on everything, but peace and civility are most important. Jesus said, *"Your love for one another will prove to the world that you are My disciples"* (John 13:35 NLT).

I read to them out of Galatians five about the deeds of the flesh. Listed among them are hostility, quarreling, jealousy, outbursts of anger, selfish ambition, dissension, division, and envy. They had exhibited all of these. I asked them why they would want to reunite with a denomination that had treated them and RRCP so badly. They really had no answer.

However, they repented with tears and prayers. We decided if the others were willing to give them another chance, we would let them continue with RRCP. We all went to the meeting with the other pastors and leaders. There were a lot of tears, hugs, and prayers for one another. We went back home thanking God for the healing of the Palawan group.

Soon after, we discovered Larry was seeking an adulterous relationship. They continued missing the pastors' meetings and fellowship gatherings. Larry and Judy were openly uniting themselves with the denomination and their ministries.

We asked the leaders to visit Larry and Judy's churches and assess them. They had become nearly nonexistent. Their church services were also full of complaints and outburst of anger. People had stopped attending.

It was finally time to take definite action. The Tagumpay churches and sheep were being scattered. The wolves in pastors' clothing had reviled themselves.

Here is what the Apostle Paul had told the elders of Ephesus. The wolves were to come from among them.

> *28 "So guard yourselves and God's people. Feed and shepherd God's flock—His church, purchased with His own blood—over which the Holy Spirit has appointed you as elders.*
>
> *29 I know that <u>false teachers, like vicious wolves, will come in among you after I leave, not sparing the flock.</u>*
>
> *30 Even some <u>men from your own group will rise up and distort the truth in order to draw a following</u>" (Acts 20:28-30 NLT).*

The church had to be protected. Sheep were being lost. Soon Pastor Alagos was again on a plane for Palawan. Circumstances prevented me from going this time.

Larry and Judy agreed to leave and vacate the church and parsonage. We forgave them a financial debt and allowed them to keep the motorcycle. However, in leaving they destroyed the CR (toilet), put holes in the walls of the church building, and knocked down the fence before they left. They offered verbal threats to harm the pastors.

After they left the church, we discovered Larry and Judy had stolen money from congregation. They had convinced people to invest in a co-op farming project. The people were setting aside money monthly and Larry and Judy were the bank. They left with all the money the people were saving.

Larry and Judy were accepted back into the denomination.

THE LORD IS BLESSING

All of the Palawan pastors and many leaders are rotating church services and visitation to the Tagumpay people. The church is beginning to stabilize and grow. Members were relieved that we took action on their behalf. The people knew that the other pastors of RRCP and Pastor Alagos and I were not like Larry and Judy. RRCP's reputation for the most part is preserved.

Because of our faith in our Lord Jesus, we know He is working this all out for His glory and the salvation of His church in Palawan. Thank you, Lord!

MY ASSESSMENT

It is unfortunate that church discipline must take place. As leaders, we cannot stand by and watch leaders destroy the Lord's Church. The Apostle Paul warned the Ephesian elders that this would take place. *"Even some men from your own group will rise up and distort the truth in order to draw a following."*

Jesus gave instruction on how to handle church discipline.

> *"If another believer sins against you, go privately and point out the offense. If the other person listens and confesses it, you have won that person back. But if you are unsuccessful, take one or two others with you and go back again, so that everything you say may be confirmed by two or three witnesses. If the person still refuses to listen, take your case to the church. Then if he or she won't accept the church's decision, treat that person as a pagan or a corrupt tax collector"* (Matthew 18:15-17 NLT).

The final solution is to take it to the church and if they do not repent, they are to be treated as a pagan or corrupt tax collector. In their time, that meant have nothing to do with them. It was effectively a dis-fellowship.

As we minister to God's Church, purchased with the Lord Jesus' blood, we must be willing to administer the whole counsel of God. It includes not only faith, forgiveness, mercy, and grace, but also discipline.

The discipline is for three reasons. One is to guard the Lord's church against those who would influence inappropriate behavior. Another is to warn the church that holy living is required. Lastly, it is so the offenders have a chance to repent.

In the Corinthian church, there was a man who had undergone church discipline. There must have come a time when he repented. Paul asked the church to forgive him and accept him back or the discipline might be too much for him.

> *"I am not overstating it when I say that the man who caused all the trouble hurt all of you more than he hurt me. Most of you opposed him, and that was punishment enough. Now, however, it is time to forgive and comfort him. Otherwise he may be overcome by discouragement. So I urge you now to reaffirm your love for him"* (1 Corinthians 2:5-8 NLT).

Larry and Judy did indeed hurt the church. Equally important is they hurt themselves. In telling the whole story, you can see they were at one time a blessing as

138

leaders in our Lord's church. Satan has taken them down. However, I believe they are not down for the count. With God's renewing love for them and our prayers, they will find their way back. Maybe or maybe not with RRCP, but I know God is not finished with them. Amen!

> *I thank Christ Jesus our Lord, who has given me strength to do his work. He considered me trustworthy and appointed me to serve him, <u>even though I used to blaspheme the name of Christ. In my insolence, I persecuted his people.</u> But God had mercy on me because I did it in ignorance and unbelief. Oh, how generous and gracious our Lord was! He filled me with the faith and love that come from Christ Jesus. This is a trustworthy saying, and everyone should accept it: <u>"Christ Jesus came into the world to save sinners"—and I am the worst of them all.</u> But <u>God had mercy on me so that Christ Jesus could use me as a prime example of his great patience with even the worst sinners. Then others will realize that they, too, can believe in him and receive eternal life.</u> All honor and glory to God forever and ever! He is the eternal King, the unseen One who never dies; he alone is God. Amen"* (1 Timothy 1:12-17)!

Tagumpay Christian Center

Candeleria House Church

AN ANGEL IN THE STORM

Pastor Willer Manares and family – Victory Christian Church Sugnod

I will build My church; and the gates of Hades will not overpower it" (Matthew 16:18b).

ABOUT SIX MONTHS AFTER WE ARRIVED, IN EARLY 2012, we got a request to build a church in Sugnod, which is in a sensitive area. By sensitive I mean an area were violence and beheading still occur from faction groups. The word Sugnod means "pile of dead bodies." It earned the name from a World War II battle. One of the last battles was fought here. The dead bodies were so great they piled them up and cremated them. Many times the name of a community tells us the strongholds we are dealing with. This barangay is still under attack both literally and spiritually, and there is much death as a result.

THE ENEMY IS ROARING

Edna grew up in Sugnod. When she was young, her family tried to start a church there. That attempt, because of political issues, resulted in the death of three of Edna's uncles. Two were beheaded, and the other was tortured to death.

Now, more than twenty years later, Edna's mom, Mrs. Rica, wanted to try to establish a church again. She was willing to donate the land for the church if we would start it and construct a church building and parsonage. Of course, we would! Thank you, Lord, for the opportunity.

THE LORD IS BLESSING

Pastor Alagos and I went to survey the opportunity. We went to the Sugnod Captain and council to seek a permit for the two night Christian Concert Crusade to launch the church. Among the council members are second generation members of the faction responsible for the uncles' deaths. They treated us with respect, but informed us that only the city could give us the permit because of recent violence and more beheadings three years earlier.

The next week we went to ask the city mayor for the permit. He agreed only if we had a police escort. The next stop was the chief of police downstairs. As we arrived, the police chief and officers were just ending a Bible study -- God's providential timing. They agreed to issue the permit and provide a police escort.

Opportunities to Bless In Jesus' Name Foundations for the Sugnod Church

The next week we went to Sugnod to plan the event. While there, I asked if I could use a toilet. In the Philippines, it is called CR or Comfort Room. I am usually embarrassed to ask, because Filipino males just find a bush, tree or wall. A public CR is not common, especially in the remote areas. I am American, however, so people make allowance for me.

Well, a neighbor provided the CR in their home. As I came out from their CR, I noticed an older couple with girls about ten and twelve. The older man did not look well. As we talked, I discovered the mother of the girls left them with their grandparents while she looked for work in Manila. The grandfather was indeed sick. He went to the doctor and was diagnosed with pneumonia in both lungs. He had a prescription, but no money to get the needed medication. We prayed for the family and provided the medications. Each time we returned, we checked on him and prayed. It was a long battle, but he recovered.

The week after our first visit, we went again to Sugnod. We walked by a bamboo house with many pieces of the bamboo walls missing. The house was also leaning to one side. I asked if we could pray for the family. As we approached, my eyes welled with tears. The poverty was so stark. About one third of the bamboo flooring was also missing. The mother had ten children and she was holding one in her arms. The baby was less than one year old.

One child was wearing only a tee shirt, black from dirt. Another was wearing underwear only, also black from dirt. The baby in her arms was naked. The other children were similarly dressed.

In situations like this, I need to walk away so I can clear my tears. I do not want them to see me crying. We prayed for the family and arranged to buy two sacks of rice (about 210 pounds) for them. We came back the following week for the crusade. The mother used the rice money to buy bamboo and build a 10x10 foot new home. Remember, this is a family of twelve. I agreed the exchange made good sense. They were so happy with their new home.

While at the crusade, we were introduced to the father of the family, who had a huge round soft growth on the back of his neck. It made it hard for him to work, as he was a laborer who carried things on his back and shoulders. We sent him to the doctor. The growth was a non-malignant tumor. The doctor removed it. Amazingly, it weighed about two pounds. The father is working now and the family is doing much better.

One of our concerns was that there was no pastor in Sugnod. Our nearest church was more than four hours away via motorcycle. During our travels to Sugnod, we discovered there was a pastor from a neighboring barangay who had a Bible study in Sugnod. He had attended the same Bible college as Pastor Alagos and Edna. We agreed he could pastor the Sugnod church. It seemed like a godly match. The pastor had a dynamic youth group that played instruments and sang. All seemed well and good; we teamed up for the launch.

SUGNOD CHRISTIAN CONCERT CRUSADE – THE LAUNCH

RRCP now had three churches to help us plant this new one. We loaded two Jeepneys, each carrying about thirty people plus equipment. The RRCP youth had prepared interpretive dances to Christian songs and a skit with a redemptive message.

We arrived a day early to go house to house and invite the barangay. Our reputation of helping the grandfather get well and providing material to build the house preceded us. The people were very receptive: we were well received in spite of the escort of sixteen very well armed police, including grenades, riot guns, and M-16 rifles.

THE ENEMY ROARED

We arrived late morning. In the afternoon, a bus from the city's Catholic church showed up. They loaded the barangay youth and went back to the city. There they indoctrinated the youth, encouraging them to go door to door and remind the Sugnod people that if they attended the crusade or the church their names would be recorded and they would not be allowed to bury their dead in the only barangay cemetery, also owned by the Catholic Church. This is typical for them wherever we start churches.

The Lord Blessed

The first night of the crusade, about a dozen of the Catholic teens who went house to house observed the concert from outside the plaza. At the end of the concert, several of these teens came forward to accept Jesus as their Lord and Savior. Many of them were baptized and are youth leaders today. The second night's response was a large crowd and additional 30 people responding to a call of salvation and repentance.

Much to our pleasant surprise, during the crusade the barangay captain announced the council's approval of River Rock Church Philippines establishing a church for their people.

Our new pastor and Edna's family followed up with those who responded and started Bible studies. Mrs. Rica completed the donation of the land and soon we would construct a church building and parsonage.

The Enemy Is Roaring - The New Pastor

Typically, along with the small allowance we give a pastor, we also build a church building and sometimes a parsonage for them. We felt good about the allowance for the new pastor because he was having trouble feeding his family, trying to live off the small offering from his other church. He had another means to work, but it involved a broken motorcycle that he didn't have enough income to repair. Truly, he was in a bad situation. We thought this was an opportunity to help each other.

Unfortunately, we hadn't had time to properly vet the pastor. All seemed well until we started getting suspicious reports about his Facebook account. The pastor had a church building and parsonage in the neighboring barangay, provided by Korean missionaries. However, he was no longer with the missionaries. They had separated. The pastor kept the church building and parsonage in the separation. This should have made us suspicious.

We had already began our church building program. The pastor was helpful in this. However, people who followed him on Facebook were reporting the he was taking money from another missionary group to build our church. Two groups -- unaware of each other -- were giving money for the same project. Also, the pastor had decided to run for election as barangay captain.

RRCP has a policy that our pastors cannot be involved in politics. We informed him of this. His decision was to test us. He also declared the church and building belong to him. He justified this by saying he supervised the construction. Later, he threaten to kill Pastor Alagos and me if we attempted to take the church from him.

We gathered twelve of our pastors and other leaders and made the four-hour motorcycle trip to Sugnod. The pastor and his wife meet us at the church to try to resolve the issue. The confrontation was not easy, but we prevailed and he left. The threats continued for some time, and he also lost the election. We were told he got in trouble with money backers of the election and had to flee for his life. *"Though I walk straight into trouble, you preserve my life, stretching out your hand to fight the vehemence of my enemies, and your right hand delivers me" (Psalm 138:7 ISV).*

THE LORD IS BLESSING

With few exceptions, the church members were relieved that the pastor left. They were aware of him collecting money from two churches. Fortunately, we had all the receipts for the materials and labor. The donated land and church building were registered to RRCP. The church members faced their first trial and the church was strengthened as a result.

Pastor Alagos and I made the commitment to be the interim pastors until we could find one qualified. This meant we would make an eleven hour round trip on small motorcycles every Saturday to hold church services. Pastor Alagos' motorcycle had a 100cc engine and mine 125cc. Truly, they were more qualified as dirt bikes than to make an eleven hour road trip.

For almost two years, we would make the weekly trip. We traveled through hot sun, monsoons, and typhoons. Typically, we left at 4:30 am and arrived home between 9 pm to midnight, depending on the weather. Rainy weather was much slower. So many times, I would arrive home soaked with my shoes full of water.

Was this the enemy roaring? There would be times he roared and times our Lord blessed. It was a wonderful time to serve our Lord. The experiences we encountered, both bad and good, were life changing. They would be the bases for both of my books.

ANGELS IN THE STORM

On one particular occasion, Pastor Alagos and Edna traveled without me to Sugnod. A typhoon came in on their way home, with torrential rain and gale-force winds.

So many times, we leaned into the sideways rain, traveling slow because of the downpour. The rain could be so thick that seeing past the front wheel of the motorcycle was difficult. We must keep moving because the towns and gas stations are closed. More than that, we both have messages to preach Sunday morning at our own churches. The ministries must continue in spite of the weather.

On one of these stormy nights, Pastor Alagos and Edna were on their way home. Pastor Alagos tells the story that his motorcycle was slowing down on its own. The more it slowed, the more he advanced the throttle to try to increase the speed. Finally, frustrated, he pulled the motorcycle over to see what the problem was. As he and Edna got off the motorcycle, they saw they had stopped just before a washed out bridge. Had they traveled just a few feet more, they would have landed in the raging water below.

In my mind's eye, I can see the angels pulling on the back of the motorcycle while Pastor Alagos leans forward, trying to increase the speed. Thank you, Lord, for sending strong angels!

> *"The angel of the LORD encamps around those*
> *who fear Him, and rescues them" (Psalm 34:7).*

For me this is just another encounter with the deliberate providence of God. Thank you, Lord, for we have so much more to do if we are willing.

PASTOR WILLER AND DIANE MANARES

After almost two years of traveling every Saturday to Sugnod, I received a communication through the internet from Pastor Willer Jun Manares, who lived far north of us on the island of Luzon. He and his wife Diane had been following us on the internet. They were helping Pastor Willer's father plant churches and were ready to move out on their own.

In the beginning, I did not think much of it, but they were persistent. Finally, I shared their letters and resume with Pastor Alagos and he called them. Pastor Alagos knew one of their mentors and was encouraged. They were living in Luzon but were from the Sugnod area. They knew the language and the culture. Could this be our new Sugnod pastor? We prayed and, after a while, we visited face to face. They were a young couple with two elementary school age boys. The Sugnod church was young couples and young teens. The Manares family was committed and eager to start.

The Sugnod church had a separate parsonage. The church and the parsonage were almost completely rebuilt after typhoon Yolanda. The fit was good and we started them in Sugnod. The church accepted them with open arms. Diane is a beautiful and godly young lady who has attracted the young girls to follow her, leading the young with grace and humility.

PASTOR WILLER

Pastor Willer has a thirst for Biblical knowledge. He is one of our most well-read pastors. Because I am 68 years old now, I am constantly aware of the eventual need to replace myself. We need well-grounded men in the Word of God to keep the church on track. Pastor Willer is one I am investing in. Our pastors come from many denominations with varying degrees of education. Most are not well educated in the Bible. They are men who are called and the Holy Spirit is strong within them. However, we all need to come to a common faith based on the Bible.

> *"Do your best to present yourself to God as an approved worker who has nothing to be ashamed of, handling the word of truth with precision"* (2Timothy 2:2 ISV).

My goal over the next two years is to teach the Bible, to give our pastors and leaders the knowledge to be able to handle the Word of God accurately, and teach what the Bible says. I pray this will ensure that, in the future, only our Lord's Gospel be proclaimed, and only His Church will be established and continue.

"And He gave some as apostles, and some as prophets, and some as evangelists, and some as pastors and teachers, <u>for the equipping of the saints for the work of service</u>, to the <u>building up of the body of Christ</u>; until we all <u>attain to the unity of the faith</u>, and of the <u>knowledge of the Son of God</u>, to <u>a mature man</u>, to the mea-sure of the stature which belongs to the fullness of Christ.

As a result, we are <u>no longer to be children, tossed here and there by waves and carried about by every wind of doctrine, by the trickery of men, by craftiness in deceitful scheming</u>; but speaking the truth in love, we are <u>to grow up in all aspects into Him who is the head, even Christ</u>, from whom the whole body, <u>being fitted and held together by what every joint supplies, according to the proper working of each individual part, causes the growth of the body for the building up of itself in love</u>" (Ephesians 4:11-16).

Our Lord is supplying us with humble, teachable, and Spirit-filled servants who are growing into the *"<u>unity of the faith, and of the <u>knowledge of the Son of God</u>, to <u>a mature man</u>, to the <u>measure of the stature which belongs to the fullness of Christ</u>."* Thank you, Lord!

Pastor Willer Jun and Diane Manares

Victory Christian Church Congregation - Sugnod

Sugnod Family

Sugnod Family New Home

OFF WITH THEIR HEADS

Victory Christian Church – Dreams and Warnings

> *"The LORD is my light and my salvation;
> Whom shall I fear? The LORD is the defense
> of my life; Whom shall I dread?*
>
> *When evildoers came upon me to devour my
> flesh, My adversaries and my enemies, they
> stumbled and fell.*
>
> *Though a host encamp against me, My heart
> will not fear; Though war arise against me, In
> spite of this I shall be confident"* (Psalm 37:1-3).

ABOUT A YEAR AFTER WE STARTED THE VICTORY
Christian Church Sugnod, we were warned that our heads
could be cut off.

Pastor Alagos and TOP were invited to a birthday party
of one of their members. This was on a Friday: the day
before our usual Saturday motorcycle ride to Sugnod to
hold a worship service. When Juliana and I arrived at the

party, there were many groups of people talking and very excited. When people saw me arrive, they began to encircle me. Juliana disappeared into one of the groups.

They began to cry and tell me that three of the church ladies had the same dream of Pastor Alagos and me being beheaded if we went to Sugnod the next day. This was unusual, as dreams and prophetic warnings like this are not a usual spiritual experience for us. This was in fact our first time.

Dreams of this sort were sometimes experienced in the book of Acts and other places. God has often warned through dreams and prophets.

> The Apostle Paul said, *"And now, behold, bound by the Spirit, I am on my way to Jerusalem, not knowing what will happen to me there, except that the Holy Spirit solemnly testifies to me in every city, saying that bonds and afflictions await me"* (Acts 20:22, 23).

> *"As we were staying there for some days, a prophet named Agabus came down from Judea. And coming to us, he took Paul's belt and bound his own feet and hands, and said, "This is what the Holy Spirit says: 'In this way the Jews at Jerusalem will bind the man who owns this belt and deliver him into the hands of the Gentiles.'" When we had heard this, we*

as well as the local residents began begging
him not to go up to Jerusalem" (Acts 21:10-12).

At first I thought we might want to cancel the next day's trip and wait for a safer time. Then a thought came to mind. We knew the dangers before we went to Sugnod to build the church. Others had already been beheaded there. Why would we stop now? The Lord had been with us starting this church and through many other dangers. He had always been faithful.

What if we only chose the safe road or safe church to plant and then died from a road accident or cancer? We can only do what our Lord has assigned to us and thank God when we know what we are to do. Not everyone knows the will of God in his or her life. *"But I do not consider my life of any account as dear to myself, so that I may <u>finish my course and the ministry which I received from the Lord Jesus</u>, to testify solemnly of the gospel of the grace of God"* (Acts 20:24).

I set out to find Pastor Alagos. When I found him, I do not know which one of us said it first: "I am going tomorrow, how about you?"

The next morning, at about 5 am, we set off for Sugnod. The weather was clear and we were making good time. Edna was riding on the back of Pastor Alagos' motorcycle as usual. All the way there, I was praying, asking God if it was His will to end my life that day. Whatever His will was, we were on our way and His will would unfold for us.

Sometimes the Lord calls for his servants to give up their lives for the greater good of the Gospel. I had this conversation with one of my elders, Dr. David W. Robinson, before we came to the Philippines. We concluded that if God asked for martyrdom He would give us the grace to do so as men of God. We would need faith in God's will and purpose. I remember I made a similar decision when I volunteered for military service in the Vietnam War. Would I be willing to give up my life for my country and not my Lord? Here is the account of Stephen: the first martyr for the sake of the Gospel.

> *"Now when they heard this, they were cut to the quick, and they began gnashing their teeth at him. But being full of the Holy Spirit, he gazed intently into heaven and saw the glory of God, and Jesus standing at the right hand of God; and he said, "Behold, I see the heavens opened up and the Son of Man standing at the right hand of God." But they cried out with a loud voice, and covered their ears and rushed at him with one impulse. When they had driven him out of the city, they began stoning him; and the witnesses laid aside their robes at the feet of a young man named Saul. They went on stoning Stephen as he called on the Lord and said, "Lord Jesus, receive my spirit!" Then falling on his knees, he cried out with a loud*

voice, "Lord, do not hold this sin against them!"
Having said this, he fell asleep" (Acts 7:54-60).

God's grace was indeed with Stephen. Our Lord showed Himself to Stephen to encourage him. The Lord Jesus watched as His servant willingly lay down his life. He watched and listened as Stephen asked Him to forgive his persecutors. I believe Jesus stood in honor of His brave and faithful servant. Jesus was not sitting at the right hand of God, but standing! *"Jesus <u>standing</u> at the right hand of God."* We all must die. Would we choose to die suffering in our bed or bravely in our Lord's service with grace and honor? Either way I pray he gives me grace for the death at hand.

While on our way, my thoughts were filled with scenarios of what might happen. My senses were heightened. The last ten kilometers of our trip is dirt road, with many places for an ambush. I was on full alert while on the dirt road. However, nothing happen. When we got to the church, still I was watching because Edna's uncles had been pulled from their home and beheaded just meters from the church. During the church service, nothing happened. Thank you, Lord!

Finally, it was time for us to start home. We had to pass by the dirt road again. I watched closely, and again nothing happen. Then we were on the paved road. I sighed with relief: we were now safe. However, I could see several men – maybe a dozen - up the road standing on both sides of the road. As we got closer, I could see they all had bolos (machetes) and hatchets. Their faces were covered with cloths. Was this a work crew? A work crew could look like this also. They were not working. In fact, they were all watching us approach.

I thought we should turn around and find another way home. It would add several hours to our trip, but would be safer. Pastor Alagos and Edna were ahead of me and not slowing down. I was not going to leave them. The closer we got to the men the more they were staring at us with weapons in hand. I prepared to head off into the rice fields should the situation turn bad.

Well, we passed through the men. All they did was watch as we came. I could see them looking at us in my mirror after we passed through.

Did our Lord protect us? Did He confuse or freeze them as we passed by? Did angels stay their hands? I will never know for sure. Nevertheless, one thing is certain: this entire situation was not coincidence! There is no such thing as coincidence: only the providence of our Lord. God's divine orchestration, not luck or coincidence, is what I see in this ministry.

Like when the King of Aram went to war against Israel. Elisha opened the eyes of his servant to show God's power. There is always more of us than of them.

> "So he answered, "Do not fear, for those who
> are with us are more than those who are with
> them." Then Elisha prayed and said, "O LORD,
> I pray, open his eyes that he may see." And

the LORD opened the servant's eyes and he saw; and behold, the mountain was full of horses and chariots of fire all around Elisha" *(2 Kings 6:16, 17).*

In my mind, I think the conversation after we passed through the men went something like this: "What happened? Were we not ready? Why did you not strike them? I thought you would hit them. How will we explain this?"

Through many trials and dangers, my Lord has delivered us. I believe it is because He not finished with us. Thank you, Lord!

Victory Christian Church

Blessings After
of the Storm

Victory Christian Church Sugnod
Super Typhoon Yolanda – (International Name: Haiyan)

WE HAD NEARLY COMPLETED THE CONSTRUCTION OF the Sugnod church and parsonage buildings when Super Typhoon Yolanda hit the Philippines in November 2013. It broke every know measurement of a typhoon ever recorded. The typhoon killed more than six thousand people throughout the Philippines.

Tacloban received most of the publicity because it was hit first. We were directly west of the eye, which came in between the upper part of our island and the lower part of the island north of us. The northern part of our island is mostly rural and isolated cities and towns. Still, lives were lost, homes destroyed, and families devastated.

I cannot blame the typhoon on Satan or God. Was it a judgement of God on a nation full of false regions, witch-craft, superstition, drugs, and corruption? Maybe. Many people want to blame God for disasters like Typhoon Yolanda, sickness, death, heartache, and sorrow.

BROKEN WORLD - BROKEN LIVES -
TYPHOON YOLANDA

For me, the truth is we live in a broken world -- we and our world are broken because of sin and rebellion against our Creator and God. Everything we want to blame on God like typhoons, earthquakes, disease, and death is caused by brokenness. We have broken lives with heart-ache, sorrow, disappointment, and injustice. The world and our lives are broken because we have rejected God; we have sinned.

God made the world perfect, with no death or any cor-ruption. In fact, God enjoyed communing with Adam and Eve in the cool evening in the Garden of Eden. However, even with all God's love in a perfect creation, Adam and Eve rebelled against God. They wanted to be "like God." When they rejected God, they rejected His wondrous life for them and His perfect goodness: His perfect creation.

We all have sinned and the punishment is just for us all. The result of our rebellion was and is death: disease, sorrow, and events like Typhoon Yolanda entered our world. Our world is no longer perfect, but broken. Likewise, our lives are broken because we have rebelled against God. We reject God and want to be our own God. Our rebel-liousness produces heartache, sorrow, and destruction of our lives and families. And yet, we blame God. I cannot. I only want my life and others' lives to be restored by God's salvation. I want to see God and His blessing restored for those who love Him and are called to His purpose. (Reference the chapters *Deliberate God* 1, 2 and 3).

Nevertheless, God promises that, in spite of our broken world and broken lives, God will work through it all to produce our good if we love Him. Thank you, Lord!

> *"For I consider that the sufferings of this present time are not worthy to be compared with the glory that is to be revealed to us. For the anxious longing of the creation waits eagerly for the revealing of the sons of God. For the creation was subjected to futility, not willingly, but because of Him who subjected it, in hope that the creation itself also will be set free from its slavery to corruption into the freedom of the glory of the children of God"* (Romans 8:18-21).

THE LORD IS BLESSING

So I prayed: "Lord, we have seen what Typhoon Yolanda can do. Please show us Your great mercy."

I find it notable that in all of our eighteen churches at that time, there was no loss of life. When my family and I woke the next morning, there was little sign that a typhoon had passed over our home. A corner of our roof was missing and there was some water damage, but the roof was very old and already in bad shape. One of our bamboo storage units was also damaged, but it too was old and already in need of repair. Yet we were just miles from the eye of the super typhoon.

However, south and north of us was terrible devastation. Homes were flattened, crops lost, the tops of trees were gone, and people were homeless and hungry. Even we were without power and communication for almost two weeks. In some places, there was no electricity for nearly six months.

While we were without communication, people and groups in the USA familiar with our work here began to organize to help. As soon as we could communicate, help poured in. Because our churches are rural, the government and organizations had trouble getting there, but we could. RRCP churches became eighteen rural distribution points to help those in need.

THE BLESSING AFTER TYPHOON YOLANDA

"Typhoon Yolanda Aid Report"

- Fed 850 families 35,000 pounds of rice.
- Had many group community dinners with rice, meat, and vegetables.
- Repaired or rebuilt 251 homes.
- Repaired five churches.
- Repaired two pastors' homes.
- Provided medical aid to numerous families.

"Aid Impact"

- The number one tearful response was, "no one has ever helped us before."
- We provided building resources. As a result, the church and community are working together to help each other to rebuild.
- Many are amazed that a church would help people outside of their congregation.
- Our churches more than doubled in attendance.
- People came to hear the Gospel that had never heard before.
- Both the unchurched and de-churched are coming to church and listening. They have seen and felt who we are, and now they wanted to know more about us. As a result, our church attendance doubled. Each week folks commit or recommit their lives to Jesus Christ.
- This impact will be long lasting. It has changed the relationship of the church and community forever.
- Strongholds are disappearing, and doors are opening.
- It has set an example for other churches, and they are responding.
- There have been more than seventy baptisms.

"God is our refuge and strength, a great help in times of distress. Therefore we will not be frightened when the earth roars, when the mountains shake in the depths of the seas, when

> *its waters roar and rage, when the mountains*
> *tremble despite their pride. Interlude" (Psalm*
> *46:1-3 ISV).*

BARANGAY SUGNOD – VICTORY CHRISTIAN CHURCH

After the typhoon, the church and parsonage's top roofs were gone. shredded like ripped sheets of paper and flung all over Sugnod. The unfinished concrete block walls were waterlogged. The barangay homes, mostly made of bamboo and nipa roofs, were devastated and flattened. Both bridges were washed away, making getting to Sugnod difficult.

The weekend after the typhoon, Pastor Alagos and I visited Sugnod. The rivers were still high so we left the motorcycles and waded through the rivers and walked in. The path is uphill from the last river. When we got to the top we stopped to rest on a bench in front of a small store to empty the water from our shoes.

There was a man there, and Pastor Alagos engaged him in conversation. He was in his forties and muscular. He was obviously a hard working guy. I did not understand the conversation until I heard the phrase "oh diyos ko," which means "oh my God." At that point, I asked Pastor Alagos what they were talking about.

The man was telling him that he had never prayed before until the typhoon. The day of the typhoon he had been standing in this very spot. He looked over and saw two houses lifted up and coconut trees uprooted and carried away. This was only twenty to thirty meters from where he stood. He said at that time he prayed and asked God to save his life. I told Pastor Alagos to invite him to church the next Sunday.

The following Sunday we delivered fifty sacks (almost six thousand pounds) of premium rice by jeepney to the barangay. Because the bridge was out, many men carried the sacks on their heads through the river, up the hill and to the other side of the barangay where the church was located. We only bought and delivered premium rice, as the government was delivering rice that had gone bad and was making people sick. Also, many times the drivers of the trucks would sell the rice instead of giving it out. Since this was from the Lord and in His name, it would need to be good rice.

Most of the families, because of poverty, had never eaten premium rice. We wanted the experience to be without criticism and to be talked about in a good way for a long time to come. I have never received a blessing from God that was not premium. Thank you, Lord. One did not need to be a member of the church to receive help. The local church leaders and barangay council determined those in need. I believe that because of our faith in blessing people in Jesus' name, not RRCP's name, our Lord increased the blessing like the loaves and fishes.

LOVE YOUR ENEMIES

The man who had prayed for our Lord to save his life was there to help distribute the food, and every Sunday thereafter for many months to come. Due to the bridges being out for several months, we could not get supplies in to rebuild the church or repair homes. As a result, we worshiped in the church with no roof. We only had a small tarp that we hung from a rope. We keep moving the tarp during the service as the sun moved.

Later, I learn that the man was the mastermind for the beheadings of Edna's uncles some twenty years earlier. Edna's mom and father were also attending the services. The family welcomed him to the church without condemnation. He stopped coming a few months later. Nevertheless, it was not because he was not loved in Jesus' name. Please pray that the man returns to church and his eternal life is saved.

> *"You have heard that it was said, 'YOU SHALL LOVE YOUR NEIGHBOR and hate your enemy.'*
> *"But I say to you, love your enemies and pray for those who persecute you, so that you may be sons of your Father who is in heaven; for He causes His sun to rise on the evil and the good, and sends rain on the righteous and the unrighteous" (Matthew 5:43-45)*

THE BLIND WOMAN

About a month after the typhoon, we had twelve baptisms in Sugnod. One of the ladies that was baptized was
in her sixties. She was blind and her ten year old granddaughter lived with her, leading grandmother wherever
she wanted to go.

Her home was one of many we decided to rebuild. The
roof was mostly gone and the home was leaning to one side.
The lady and granddaughter were sleeping under the table
in the kitchen to keep the rain off them. It would be weeks
before we could get building materials to the barangay.

The night of the baptisms, we had a worship and
praise service. Many gave testimonies about how God was
blessing their lives in spite of the typhoon. One of the big
blessings was that no one was hurt or killed. That in itself
was a miracle!

The lady gave her testimony. Even though she was
sleeping under her table, she said she felt a peace that
she had never felt before. She knew that God was making
everything right.

> *"Be anxious for nothing, but in everything by*
> *prayer and supplication with thanksgiving let*
> *your requests be made known to God. And the*
> *peace of God, which surpasses all comprehen-*
> *sion, will guard your hearts and your minds*
> *in Christ Jesus" (Philippians 4:6, 7).*

Our eighteen churches became distribution points of food, medical help, and home repair. They became opportunities to love people in Jesus' name. The stories of Sugnod are multiplied eighteen times. I am sure they are multiplied like the loaves and fishes. We were given the opportunity to see many blessings. However, the Lord's blessing are multilayered and multi-faceted and more than we can understand. I am sure they are generational as well. I am in awe to be a small part of the mercy of God.

My prayer was, "Lord, we have seen what Super Typhoon Yolanda can do. Lord, please show us Your great mercy."

Victory Christian Church after Typhoon Yolanda

Yolanda Food Distribution

Typhoon Yolanda Rice Distribution

STORIES OF FAITH AND ENCOURAGEMENT

Twenty-Eight Day Feeding Program

In 2015, I was introduced to a fellow missionary, Brother Paul Wilson, who had been in the Philippines for nearly thirty years. He lives on Negros Island, next to our Panay Island. In his time here, he has planted more than a hundred churches. Paul has turned out to be an amazing inspiration and resource.

Feeding Malnourished Children

In the past, we were able to have a weekly feeding program in each of our twenty-eight churches. After a few years, the funding for the program began to fade out. It was a small group of individual donors. I began looking for a resource to keep the feeding program going. Although I have not be able to fund the program fully, Paul did tell me of an organization that could help in a different way. The organization is called ICM or International Care Ministries. Their purpose is to provide hygiene, health training, and livelihood training and resources.

ICM works together with Stop Hunger Now and Harvest Pack. Both organizations provide nutritional food formulated to help malnourishment. I wrote ICM and began to ask questions about getting their food packs for our feeding program. Well, the weekly feeding program did not fit their ministry. However, helping malnourished children did. As it turns out, they had an extra supply of food packs both on our island and Palawan. They had Stop Hunger Now food packs here on Panay and Harvest Pack ones on Palawan.

ICM said that if we could feed the food daily for one month, we could bring a child out of malnourishment. We had already experienced that even one nutritious feeding weekly made a big difference for a child. Therefore, feeding daily for a month made a lot of sense.

Because of my relationship with Pastor Alagos and the elementary schools, I knew they were all battling poor performance levels from the moderately to severely malnourished children. Most cannot read or do simple math. Our experience with CCC taught us that the combination of tutoring and nutritious meals would bring most children up to grade level. Many, once helped, excelled.

Along with food, we provide teachers who love and believe the children can do well, and much can be accomplished. In addition, we teach them hygiene, nutrition, and values. They are introduced to God and His love for them. They are loved by the sponsors who provide for their needs, the teachers, and the God who created them. The parents, who are in most cases illiterate, also come to realize His love for them and their children.

With twenty-eight churches now, I calculated food packs for forty-two malnourished children per church to be fed once per day for twenty-eight consecutive days. That is 1,176 children fed for twenty-eight days --32,928 meals!

ICM agreed to provide the food. All we had to do was pick it up.

So now the logistics. Bringing the children to the church daily was difficult, as school was about to begin. We asked the pastors, school principals, and barangay officials to help us identify those most in need and to help us gather the children and feed them daily. We already had some experience in organizing aid from Super Typhoon Yolanda. In some barangays we fed from the church, others were fed at school, and still others were fed by the barangay at their plaza.

The program was very successful. In barangay Minoro the children, ages one to eleven years old, gained an average weight of 3.6 kilos or 7.9 pounds. In a few cases children doubled their weight. The results were similar throughout our twenty-eight churches and their associated barangays and elementary schools.

"When it was evening, the disciples came to Him and said, "This place is desolate and the hour is already late; so send the crowds away, that they may go into the villages and buy food for themselves." <u>But Jesus said to them, "They do not need to go away; you give them something to eat!"</u> They said to Him, "We have here only five loaves and two fish." And He said, "Bring them here to Me." Ordering the people to sit down on the grass, He took the five loaves and the two fish, and looking up toward heaven, He blessed the food, and breaking the loaves

He gave them to the disciples, and the disciples gave them to the crowds, <u>*and they all*</u>
<u>*ate and were satisfied.*</u> *They picked up what*
was left over of the broken pieces, twelve full
baskets" (Matthew 14:16-20).

Jesus was concerned for those who were following Him.
They were hungry. Jesus told the disciples to feed them
When they stepped out in faith, He blessed the efforts of
the disciples and the food. The people were fed and satisfied. Their needs were met.

- Jesus was concerned for the welfare of the followers.
- He made the disciples aware and commissioned
  them to minister to the people. *"Give them some-*
  thing to eat!"
- The disciples discovered their resources. *"We have*
  here only five loaves and two fish."
- The resources were not enough.
- God blessed their faith and their resources. *"They*
  all ate and were satisfied."
- Their resources and God's blessing were more than
  enough. *"What was left over of the broken pieces,*
  twelve full baskets."

How awesome it is to be a part of God's care for people!
How awesome it is to see those suffering loved and cared
for! Thank you, Lord, for allowing us to be a part of
your love.

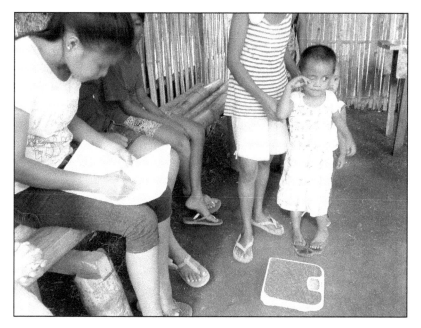

Recording the Effectiveness of the program

Thank You Lord!

Experiencing Poverty

"When they saw us coming, they had hope."

ONE DAY, WE WENT TO PRAY FOR A FAMILY THAT HAD a miscarriage in the seventh month. The baby was a boy. Two of our Grace Chapel youth were from this family. Just a few days before, these two youth were recipients of clothes and school supplies sent from our home church in the USA.

It was rainy season. We walked into the mountainous part of Dacutan, where Grace Chapel is. Juliana, six of our Grace Chapel ladies, and Pastor Jojo and I went to pray for them and give a love offering. Our travel was a muddy footpath, wading across a river, and walking an old bamboo hanging bridge.

I am a large American and the Filipinos who walk this bridge weigh considerably less. It was faith that God would protect me that caused me to step out on the bridge. Thanks to Him, I made it to the other side. The mud path had sugarcane stalks and sticks covering it so our feet would not sink too deep. I had seen school children come from this area carrying their shoes to keep the mud from them.

As we walked the path to their home, many people joined us. Some of the community members and the family said that when they saw us coming, they had hope. We finally arrived at the bamboo home. You could see easily through the walls, and it was leaning and in need of repair.

A few of us stepped inside. The mother was sitting on the bamboo floor, also with many missing pieces. You could see she was very weak, her eyes full of tears at our sight. Beside her was a cardboard box with the dead baby boy wrapped in a blanket inside. His small face was showing. Near the box, on the floor, was a single small candle lit as a symbol of mourning. The father was off preparing the grave at the local public cemetery.

The ladies were quick to make sure the mother was okay, offer words of sympathy, and check to see that she and the children were safe. The family had no money for a doctor or medicine. We prayed for her healing.

I observed several of the children were malnourished. Four of their children come to the Grace Chapel feeding program on Saturdays. Sometimes they show up at our home, and we feed them.

The mother was 38, and this was her tenth child. The father helped deliver the already dead baby. He had to push the baby out. If he had not been brave, maybe the mother would have died during delivery. We prayed she would have no infection. Pastor Jojo offered a prayer of healing and comfort. The ladies continued to speak with the mother and tried to help with the words from their hearts.

As I walked home, my thoughts were about how blessed my family and I are. I thanked God for our health, our home, and the means He has given us to care for ourselves and others.

Also in my heart, I was trying to understand the helplessness they must feel. It is their daily life. In spite of their poverty, the Filipinos are an enduring people. When I see the children, they are smiling, clean, and well mannered.

Oh Lord, help us to bring hope and love to the Filipino people wherever You establish us.

POST SCRIPT

The mother went to the medical clinic. They used our love offering for medication. She is now in good health. Thank you, Lord!

The oldest of their children, a teenage girl Hanny, has since come to live with us. She is a blessing to Juliana, helping around the house. With the money she earns from us she can continue in school and help her family.

There are too many like this in the Philippines. I have been told 30% of Filipino children are malnourished. There is so very much more we can do.

The Good Shepherd says *"I will feed My flock and I will lead them to rest,"* declares the Lord GOD. *"I will seek the lost, bring back the scattered, bind up the broken and strengthen the sick; but the fat and the strong I will destroy. I will feed them with judgment"* (Ezekiel 34:15, 16).

I Call Her Haners

THIS STORY IS ABOUT HANNY MAE SATURNINO, THE girl mentioned in the story above. Juliana calls her Annie or Ann. I call her Haners.

Several years ago, I wrestled with the fact that I cannot help everyone. The poverty and suffering around me is harsh and breaks my heart continuously. As I have said before, so many times I have to walk away so I can clear away my tears. I pray I never become accustomed to it or stop seeing the suffering.

Someone shared with me with me that I could not help everyone. That is true. However, there are some, with the Lord's help, I can. So I focus on those the Lord brings into my path and into my heart. There are many. Thank you, Lord Jesus. The story of Haners is about one the Lord brought into my path and into my heart.

Haners is the oldest child of the family mentioned in the previous story. When her mother miscarried, Haners had already been coming to Grace Chapel. When we approached the home to pray for her mother and family, I could see her sitting in her bedroom through the missing pieces of outside walls.

Our first year here in 2011, I was preaching at Grace Chapel. Haners and some of her siblings also attended.

At that time, we fed the children and adults who came to church nutritious meals. She was thirteen at the time and was hard to miss. She is pretty, with a big smile and eyes that look directly at you. Shortly thereafter, I discovered she is intelligent, determined, and willing to work hard to accomplish something with her life. One of the things I like most about her is she is always helping her family

Not only was I noticing her at church, but she and a girl friend were showing up on the weekends doing chores around our house. They came looking for food. Juliana would have them do cleaning in exchange. Soon it was just Haners showing up. Juliana not only provided food for Haners, but also some to take home for her family, plus a little allowance as well. Haners was a hard-working, honest girl.

Soon we needed her to come on Friday nights. Not long after, she would stay with us a night or two. Haners was also active with the Grace Chapel youth. Eventually, Haners was staying with us every weeknight and visiting her family on the weekends. Juliana pays her an allowance and also helps with the cost of school projects, transportation to school, lunch and uniforms. She is a member of the family and a big help and blessing to us, especially Juliana.

Am I singing her praises? I guess I am. Not everyone we try to help is a success story. We have had our hearts broken many times trying to help, only to find they do not appreciate it or even dislike us later. I will not let those discourage me. There are also the ones whose lives we have made a positive difference in both spiritually and in quality of life.

I also noticed her dedication to her schoolwork. Almost two years ago, I asked Haners how her school grades were doing. As usual, she said okay. I began asking to see her grades at the end of each semester. In the beginning, her grades were around 81-83. Not bad. One day I asked her what she wanted to do with her life. She said she wanted to take hotel & restaurant management at the local university.

I was pleased she wanted to go to college but disappointed in the degree program she chose. It made sense though, because it is the least expensive for a four-year degree. As I have observed, many students choose that one. I estimate that maybe 5,000 students per year graduate with that degree but cannot find a job. After all, how many motels are there in the Philippines: a third world country? Certainly not enough to fill all those jobs. Most colleges have the course.

I asked Haners what she would want to study if she had the money for whatever she wanted. Her answer was nursing. That makes sense as she doctors our pets and cleans wounds for us and others. She also helps take care of Tatay, Juliana's father. He is 93 years old and needs complete care. She loves it.

Therefore, I told her she needs to bring her grades up and I will see if there is a sponsor or sponsors for her. Every semester she has improved her grades. The last report card her average was 92.44. She is ending her senior year and excited for college.

I told Haners' story to a few potential sponsors and their responses were favorable.

THE ENEMY ROARING

The enemy roaring was poverty. Haners thought her only option would be the cheapest college degree. Actually, she probably thought she had no chance at college due to finances.

THE LORD IS BLESSING

- Haners as a young girl, although she did not really believe in God at the time, still prayed for a good life, including college.
- The Lord put in her a determination to work hard.
- He put in her the hope for a better life.
- The Lord created her with honesty and self-determination.
- The Lord brought us to the Philippines.
- The Lord put Haners in my and Juliana's heart.
- Although she is a little shy, the Lord put a light in her for others to see.

Haners found our Lord and was baptized. She knows He is real now. A Bible sits by her bed, and she is reading it. She now has hope and faith. I believe our Lord will follow through with Haners and she will shine His light in her life.

Thank you, Lord, that we have been able to help hundreds. And thank you, Lord, that we can help Haners. Thank you, Lord, that she has brightened our lives, and we have seen you work in her. You are an awesome God!

"Therefore, having been justified by faith, we have peace with God through our Lord Jesus Christ, through whom also we have obtained our introduction by faith into this grace in which we stand; and we exult in hope of the glory of God. And not only this, but we also exult in our tribulations, knowing that tribulation brings about perseverance; and perseverance, proven character; and proven character, hope; <u>and hope does not disappoint, because the love of God has been poured out within our hearts through the Holy Spirit who was given to us</u>" (Romans 5:1-5).

Hanny Mae Saturnino

Prayer for a New Baby

They got up early the next morning and wor-
shipped in the LORD's presence, and then
they returned and came to their house at
Ramah. Elkanah had marital relations with
his wife Hannah, and the LORD remembered
her. By the time of the next year's sacrifice,
Hannah had become pregnant and had borne
a son. She named him Samuel because she
said, "I asked the LORD for him" (1 Samuel
1:19, 20 ISV).

BEFORE I CAME TO THE PHILIPPINES, I DID NOT BELIEVE
in miracles like healing and direct, immediate answers
to prayer. I believed they were done in Bible times, but
they were not available for us today except in very special
circumstances. I quoted James often, but really did not
believe it.

"Is anyone among you sick? Then he must call
*for the elders of the church and **they are to***
pray over him, anointing him with oil
in the name of the Lord; and the prayer
offered in faith will restore the one who

> *is sick,* *and the Lord will raise him up, and*
> *if he has committed sins, they will be for-*
> *given him. Therefore, confess your sins to*
> *one another, and pray for one another so that*
> *you may be healed.* **The effective prayer of**
> **a righteous man can accomplish much"**
> *(James 5:14-16).*

Because James is very clear about elders praying for the sick resulting in healing, I would obey and pray, but always added "your will be done," because I did not believe our Lord would heal. I hoped the *"prayer of a righteous man can accomplish much,"* but prayed without believing.

I was about to learn something much different in the mission field.

Just before we came to the Philippines, I was in an elder's meeting at our American church. Most of the elders there had a similar view to mine about miracles. A young man and his wife were brought to the meeting. The elder and wife of the young man were concerned for him. The man was in youth ministry and he and his wife were recently married.

The young man was having bizarre thoughts. We asked him to share them and it was not long before we were confronted with obvious evil thinking. I asked the young man if he would confess Jesus as his Lord. We were immediately confronted with many demonic presences coming from the young man. They manifested themselves in hideous voices, violent threats, and gruesome facial expressions. We all in unison jumped from our chairs and laid hands on the youth, praying with all we knew to do, invoking the name of our Lord Jesus and commanding the evil ones to leave.

It was an extended battle, but in the end, they all left at once, leaving the young man at peace. His face went from gruesome to serene in an instant. Then suddenly he began to pray the most wonderful prayers of praise to our Lord with thanksgiving for his release. The young man is now serving our Lord full time as an adult with blessed ministries.

This deliverance through prayer was a precursor to what God would reveal about Himself in the mission field. God's supernatural power through prayer and the Holy Spirit are needed to advance His Church. God is alive and active, and His potency is not diminished. In fact, if anything, as Jesus' second coming approaches, His power is more available to show the wonders of His mighty name through the working of miracles and the powerful answering of prayer. The Apostle Paul tells us,

> *"Finally, **be strong in the Lord and in the strength of His might**. Put on the full armor of God, so that you will be able to stand firm against the schemes of the devil. For our struggle is not against flesh and blood, but against the rulers, against the powers, against the world forces of this darkness, against the*

> *spiritual forces of wickedness in the heavenly*
> *places" (Ephesians 6:10-12).*

I find we can be strong in the Lord and operate in His strength and might. I often experience His strength and His might. That is the point of this book. Even though the enemy throws everything he has at us to thwart us in ministry, God is working powerfully to accomplish His will: establishing His Church. If we are operating in His will, He brings the victory. God is not indecisive, but works powerfully with glory and majesty.

My dear friend Paul Wilson was taught like I was about miracles. However, as we became acquainted, I told him the stories of healings and answering prayer directly and in such ways that we knew the answers were from Him.

About ten months ago, Pastor Jojo and I went to visit Paul at his home to see his ministry. A Filipino pastor and wife live with Paul and his wife, helping them in the ministry. As we were about to leave Paul called the pastor's wife and others to say good-bye to us.

As we were gathered, Paul explained that the pastor and his wife had been married seven years with no children. They had tried many doctors to no avail. Paul continued to explain the miracles and answers to prayer that RRCP was experiencing. Then Paul asked that Pastor Jojo and I pray that she would conceive and have a child.

We prayed that our Lord would open her womb and allow her to conceive a blessed child. Like with Hannah, we asked that the child would be a special child who would bring honor and glory to His name. We dedicated the child to Him. In addition, we asked that the Lord would do this immediately and in such a way that it would bring glory and honor to His name and that all would know that He is God and there is no other.

About six weeks later, we got an email from Paul that the lady was pregnant. A few weeks ago, she had a son named Kent. Our Lord is awesome and powerful, and His potency is not diminished by time, history, or misinterpretation of scripture. He does whatever He wants to bring honor and glory to His name. Moreover, He hears the prayers of His servants who minister in His name and His will.

I am excited to see what our Lord does with the life of this blessed child.

> *"The effective prayer of a righteous man can accomplish much. Elijah was a man with a nature like ours, and he prayed earnestly that it would not rain, and it did not rain on the earth for three years and six months. Then he prayed again, and the sky poured rain and the earth produced its fruit" (James 16b-18).*

I pray that you and I would become more confident in our prayers so the glory of God may be revealed through His faithful servants.

"Then the disciples came to Jesus privately and said, "Why could we not drive it out?" And He said to them, "<u>Because of the littleness of your faith</u>; for truly I say to you, if you have faith the size of a mustard seed, you will say to this mountain, 'Move from here to there,' and it will move; and nothing will be impossible to you" (Matthew 17:19, 20). AMEN!*

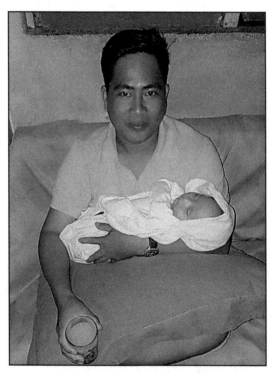

Miracle Baby Brent and Daddy

LEARNING TO HEAR GOD

ONE MORNING, THE THOUGHT CAME TO ME THAT I would be the one to preach at Grace Chapel that afternoon. I thought maybe I could preach the message I preached last week at a different church: *HAPPY TOGETHER*. It is a good message I would like Grace Chapel to hear. Then I had another thought: No. You need to preach the message before that one: *LOVE YOUR ENEMIES*. I thought, but Lord, Jojo is their pastor. He will have a message already. Lord, should I ask him to let me preach? After that, I had no more thoughts of that conversation.

**Later that morning,
Pastor Jojo asked if I could preach at Grace Chapel
that afternoon...**

I told Pastor Jojo of my thoughts with God earlier, and we both praised God with laughter of joy at the awesome God we have.

That afternoon, the time for the service arrived. However, we had torrential rain from the coming typhoon, and no one had shown up for the service. I prayed, "God, you moved so much to have me here, and now this rain?"

Then, slowly people started to arrive. Eventually, we had more people than usual and even a new person. Still, the heavy rain would not let up. We have a steel roof on the Chapel, and when the heavy rain hits it, you can hear nothing else. We waited and waited. Finally, Juliana said I would need to use my big voice.

I prayed again. "Lord forgive inn foi iny sins, and anoint this worship service so your Word may be heard!"

As I approached the podium, the rain stopped. The closing of the message came and just at the end of the prayer, the torrential rain hit again.

Powerful, Mighty, Majestic, Awesome, and Sovereign is our God! I love serving our Lord!

Here Is a Summary of the Message.

COURAGEOUS LOVE – LOVE YOUR ENEMIES

"But I SAY, LOVE YOUR ENEMIES! [Bless those who curse you. Do good to those who hate you.] Pray for those who persecute you" *(Matthew 5:44)!*

It is only possible to love our enemies through Jesus Christ. The command to love our enemies is only fully understood through the cross.

Loving your enemies is a central theme of the Bible; love through the cross. We were the enemies of God because of our sins and rebellion. Jesus died for us while we were enemies. It was our sin that caused all of His sufferings. Our sin that resulted in scourging Him bloody almost to death, our sin that stayed Him on the cross, our sin that mocked Him in His suffering. While suffering for our rebellious sin He said, "Forgive them."

It was our sin and His love to forgive us that caused Him to hold Himself on the cross and suffer our complete penalty until His last breath. This was His demonstration of His love for us in order that we could become enemies no more, but transformed to become His beloved children. But it was not possible until Jesus loved us through the cross!

> *"FOR IF WHILE WE WERE ENEMIES WE WERE RECONCILED TO GOD BY THE DEATH OF HIS SON, MUCH MORE, NOW THAT WE ARE RECONCILED, SHALL WE BE SAVED BY HIS LIFE" (Romans 5:10) [Capitalized by me for emphasis].*

Only His Church, you and I, who have experienced such undeserved courageous love of selfless sacrifice from our Lord through His great suffering and death, can understand the grandeur of God's love. Only after experiencing such grand love can we, the church, show this remarkable love to others. We show love not just to our friends, but to those undeserving of our love: our enemies.

We are called to be the light of God into a dark, lost, and dying world. How great is the light of our Lord, who loves and sacrificed Himself for the undeserving: you and me. In like manner, how great is His light as it shines through us, loving sacrificially and courageously a world undeserving who are enemies of God and even us.

It takes courage to reach out and love someone who is our enemy. Courageous was our Lord's love for us. Courageous is our love, not just to love those who love us, but also our enemies.

> *"Therefore be imitators of God, as beloved children; and walk in love, just as Christ also loved you and gave Himself up for us, an offering and a sacrifice to God as a fragrant aroma" (Ephesians 5:1).*

Has our Lord put someone on your heart to love sacrificially: courageously? Be courageous and love them.

I believe the Lord wanted me to preach this message on a particular day to a particular people. There was a heart or hearts that needed to hear about God's forgiveness and how to forgive. Because I listened to the small voice in my heart, those who needed to hear the message heard it. As I prepared the message at an earlier time, I heard God speaking through His Word this message of forgiveness. Because Pastor Jojo listens to God, he asked me to preach that day. Because the people who heard the message listened to the prompting of God to come to church in spite of the storm, they heard it.

- The Lord speaks through a small voice -- the Holy Spirit.
- He speaks through His Word.
- He speaks through others.
- He speaks through circumstance.

It is through the training of our heart that we come to discern the voice of the Lord and through obedience, we and others are blessed.

I believe blessings come through hearing and obeying. Lives are enriched. Maybe, because of your listening to God to read this account, the blessings continue.

> *So He said, "Go forth and stand on the mountain before the LORD." And behold, the LORD was passing by! And a great and strong wind was rending the mountains and breaking in pieces the rocks before the LORD; but the LORD was not in the wind. And after the wind an earthquake, but the LORD was not in the earthquake. After the earthquake a fire, but the LORD was not in the fire; <u>and after the fire a sound of a gentle blowing. When Elijah heard it</u>... (1 Kings 19:11-13).*

THE WITCH

VERY SOON AFTER WE ARRIVED CAME OUR FIRST roaring of the enemy, by way of a young, powerful, and cunning witch.

When we first arrived, we were like babes in the woods: "fresh off the boat," so to speak. We were innocent and unsure what the ministry would look like. We were hopeful with great expectation. For nearly ten years, our Lord had prepared us for the mission as a family. We were devoted to each other and to God. The elders of our home church had laid hands on us, appointing us to the Philippines' mission field to plant new churches.

We live in a rural farming community. Our home was old and in need of repair but comfortable by Filipino standards. We had no working toilet and no hot water. The water was undrinkable, and many days per week, we went without. The electricity was spotty at best. We bathed from a barrel of water with a ladle. The roof was steel and, in the hot Filipino sun, radiated heat into the home like an oven. Coming from a moderate American northwest climate to the tropical Filipino humidity and heat was almost a deal breaker. Although I had visited twice before, I really was not prepared for such a change. We were a little disoriented and in shock, I think.

It was a perfect time to put us under attack. We were adapting and making the best of things. However, small arguments started over nothing. Slowly, the tension increased in the home. It was out of character for us. Really, we were committed and knew the sacrifices we would make and we were very willing to endure for the sake and privilege of serving our Lord.

What was obvious was the stress of the new environment. Yet, it should not have caused this kind of tension in our relationships. The anger and words were not like us at all. We were beginning to think about moving home and maybe separation as a family. We had worked so long and prepared so hard for this opportunity -- I could see it falling apart, and it seemed I could do nothing to stop it.

Then someone told me our neighbor was a witch. I had never experienced witchcraft before this. Growing up as a teen, some of my friends were into witchcraft but I never really gave it much thought or credence. The Bible is full of demonic activity. As Americans we are sheltered from all this and call them myths or urban legends. It is not so in third world countries. Demonic activity, witchcraft, and the like are prevalent.

In the Philippines, a witch is called Albularyo. Their spells are called Kulam. Not too far from us is a barangay that has a festival dedicated to these practices. They are in the Filipino elementary textbooks as real people and powers.

Well, after being informed about this young neighbor woman, I began to observe. She came to our home every day. She formed a close relationship with Juliana by way of grooming her hair and giving her manicures, pedicures, and massages. This was the only time Juliana was happy. The rest of the time was anger, bad words, and chaos. We were all out of character in this.

Also, the witch was leaving her grooming appliances here -- different things in each of the rooms of our home. The pedicure things were in one room, the manicure items in another, and so on. WHY? I believe each of these, in some way, were a part of her spells.

I tried to confront Juliana several times about the witch, but arguments only increased. I was at my end. All seemed lost.

One day in desperation, I got in my car and went to visit Pastor Alagos to see if he could help. As I was on my way, the thought hit me. It was as if God said, "You have not asked me to help." It was true. I prayed much, but never directly asked God to help me.

I remembered Sister Tina at a nearby resort once told me she had a prayer room. I turned the car around and was off to the prayer room. When I got there, I asked Sister Tina if I could use it. She walked me upstairs to the room with a balcony.

When she left, I lay face down and began to pray. I told the Lord I did not know what or how to pray for this. Then this verse came to me: *"In the same way, the Spirit also helps us in our weakness, since we do not know how to pray as we should. But the Spirit himself intercedes for us with groans too deep for words, and the one who searches our hearts knows the mind of the Spirit, for the Spirit inter-cedes for the saints according to God's will" (Romans 8:26, 27 ISV).*

I asked the Holy Spirit to intercede for me. Almost instantly, I felt a peace come over me. I thought, how could this be? You need to continue to pray. But the peace of God was with me. I stood up, amazed and a little per-plexed, but absolutely at peace. After all, how long does it take the Spirit to talk with God and Him to answer? I knew God understood my prayer. It was in His hands now. I no longer had fear but serene peace. I was only in the prayer room minutes and now it was time to go home.

That night, as it became dark, two ladies, a pastora (lady pastor) and her helper, came to our home. The pas-tora explained she did not know why she was there, espe-cially at night, because it was dangerous for her to travel at night. She thought maybe it was to meet us, the new missionary family, and introduce herself.

We sat and talked. I noticed Juliana sat very close to her and was extremely attentive to the pastora. We vis-ited for a while and then she announced she needed to go. Juliana insisted I take her home.

The pastora asked if she could pray for us. As we stood, Juliana held her hand. The Pastora prayed with power and conviction, denouncing witches and witchcraft. She prayed for the peace of God and the presence of God in our home and in our ministry. It was a powerful prayer and I could feel the presence of God. When she finished the prayer, there was a peace in the house: the same overwhelming peace I experience earlier when I prayed for God's help.

As I was taking her home, she said again she had no idea why she was there -- only that God told her to go and He would protect her travel at night. She thought it strange that her prayer was singularly about a witch and deliverance.

I told her our story and she said it all made sense to her now. When I got home, all was back to normal. The curse was broken.

However, the witch still lived next to us. I prayed the Lord would remove her. I tacked on that I didn't care how she was removed from us: only that He would. Days later, Juliana informed me the witch was sick and may die. She needed to go to her home several hours away, in a town known for its witchcraft.

I was happy she was gone but repentant that the Lord would take her life. I asked the Lord to spare her life, but asked that she never return. In fact, I told the Lord that I would be willing to give my life for her if it meant she would be saved. She is well now and lives a great distance from us. She has never returned to our home.

> "My God, my rock, in whom I take refuge, My shield and the horn of my salvation, my strong-hold and my refuge; My savior, You save me from violence. I call upon the LORD, who is worthy to be praised, And I am saved from my enemies'" (2 Samuel 22:3, 4).

Never Too Late

The Anointing
Pastor Purdencio Alagos – Pastor Dionisio Oab Sr. – The
Palawan Tribes

> *"You love justice and hate wickedness. That is why God, even your God, has anointed you rather than your companions with the oil of gladness" (Psalm 45:7).*

AS WE EXITED THE VAN, TEARS WELLED UP IN EACH OF our eyes, some crying uncontrollably. None of us expected this. For us, it was an opportunity to visit a tribal pastor who needed encouragement. However, it was to be much more.

Pastor Purdencio Alagos is the father of Sarah Mahusay and brother of Pastor Alagos. Pastor Purdencio was also expelled by the denomination because of his passion to build churches for the remote communities. The denomination's goal is for cities only. As Pastor Purdencio learned about our ministry and observed how we respected his daughter and son-in-law, he became interested in joining us. Truly, he is an evangelist, responsible for many of the churches in Palawan.

Pastor Purdencio's friend is Pastor Dionisio Oab from the Palawan Sabang Tribe. He was a tribal pastor for more than twenty years, but had become discouraged and stopped pastoring. However, he did continue with a family Bible study in his home.

THE ENEMY IS ROARING

The enemy roared in Pastor Oab's life, leaving him disheartened and depressed for several years. He was a gateway into the other tribes. Many Christians abused this and took advantage of him and his people. The abusers made promises to help the tribes, but they didn't keep them. They just wanted pictures and stories to write. The Christian pastors and organizations gained publicity and donations, but the money to help never came to the tribal peoples.

THE LORD IS BLESSING

Pastor Purdencio visited Pastor Oab and assured him that not all Christians and churches are like what he experienced. Pastor Purdencio told the growing story of RRCP: Christians that come in the Lord Jesus Christ's name, establish His Churches with His salvation, and demonstrate His love.

A few months later, Pastor Alagos and I visited Palawan. We were there to encourage and see the new churches and visit potential churches. We scheduled a visit with Pastor Oab at his home. There he had gathered his family and others from the Buenavista Barangay for a worship service. One of our pastors, traveling with us, was scheduled to preach. It was his turn as we rotated speakers with each visit. There were about ten pastors and church leaders traveling in the van.

When we arrived at Buenavista, the van stopped and the side door opened. As we exited the van, we each began crying: some aloud, others wiping the continuous stream of tears. We could not stop. We were overwhelmed with an anointing of the Holy Spirit. This experience was new to us all. While walking through the very poor fishing village, we cried and asked each other what we were feeling. We each said we were experiencing the presence of our Lord. We were all in amazement at the unfolding event.

When we arrived at Pastor Oab's home, it too was filled with worshippers crying and praising God. Hands were raised and now voices became louder, singing and speaking thankful prayers to our Lord. Others were on their knees repenting and asking for forgiveness. I did not recognized speaking in angelic tongues, but serious repenting and praising God were taking place.

Even though I do not speak their language, I understood what was happening. Pastor Alagos and others confirmed what was going on. Could I have been the recipient of the language of tongues like when the church doors opened at the day of Pentecost? *"They were amazed and astonished, saying, "Why, are not all these who are speaking Galileans? And how is it that we each hear them in our own language to which we were born?"* (Acts 2:7, 8) It was not so much language that I was hearing, but I understood what they were saying and what was taking place.

Pastor Alagos was particularly affected by the experience. He was crying aloud and profusely. The scheduled speaker told me he felt the Holy Spirit had given Pastor Alagos the message for us. It was indeed true. Pastor Alagos led us all to repentance and spiritual healing before the Lord. NEVER have I had a group experience like this before or after even until now. I have experienced tears and the overwhelming presence of God in personal devotions, but not in a church experience. It was new to all of us.

I believe true healing came for Pastor Oab. His broken heart was healed before the Lord and in the presence of the Buenavista church. We were there with the sensitivity to minister to Pastor Oab. Injustice and wicked behavior had discouraged him. We were all filled and anointed with the gladness and joy of the Lord that comes to the healing of the broken hearted. *"You love justice and hate wickedness. That is why God, even your God, has anointed you rather than your companions with the oil of gladness"* (Psalm 45:7).

Soon after, Super Typhoon Yolanda hit the Philippines. This was, once again, a chance to show God's love to the poorest of the poor. Thousands of pounds of rice, clothing, blankets and household items were given in Jesus' name. The promises to love them were kept. The name of the Lord Jesus was glorified. We all thanked God and worshiped.

There are now four tribal churches and three pastors ministering to the many of the Palawan Tribes. This year Pastor Oab was ordained as a pastor.

Pastor Oab had experienced years of broken promises. Now a man in his late fifties, he was discouraged to the point of giving up. However, it is never too late for God to heal the brokenhearted and restore them to life. In Pastor Oab's case, he was restored to serving our Lord with a renewed heart of passion and gladness.

> *"Therefore repent and return, so that your sins may be wiped away, in order that times of refreshing may come from the presence of the Lord" (Acts 3:19).*

Pastor Dionisio Oab

Yes! We Will Go!

Pastor Antonio and Teodora Lachica Jr. –
The Anini-y Church

"Then I heard the voice of the Lord, saying,
'Whom shall I send, and who will go for Us?'
Then I said, 'Here am I. Send me'" (Isaiah 6:8)!

Pastor Lachica and Teodora

AFTER WE ARRIVED IN THE PHILIPPINES, WE PUT OUR son in a Christian elementary school that helps foreign students adjust to the new language and culture. It was there we met Pastor Lachica and his wife and partner in ministry, Teodora. I say wife and partner because they are inseparable, both in life and ministry. Like most Filipino pastors, they ride a motorcycle for their transportation. They are always together, even on the most difficult mountain trails, to visit churches. Through hot sun, heavy rain, and storms, they ride together serving our Lord.

I met Teodora first. Her granddaughter also attended our son's school. Many of the parents, including us, stayed at the school during the day to help meet the needs of our children. It does not take long to get to know each other.

Soon, Pastor Lachica showed up and we began getting to know each other. He was a church planter with his denomination (not the one giving us problems).

He began asking many questions about our doctrine. He knows his Bible well and has great recall of scripture. As we talk, he always relates appropriate scripture to our conversations --I love it! I did not know it at the time, but he was frustrated with his denomination. He has one purpose: to plant new churches. The denomination was too caught up in positions with titles and greater pay.

Like the church at Ephesus in Revelation, they had wandered away from their first love: Jesus. They were productive in church work but had drifted away from their Lord and Christ. They were no longer doing what the church is to do. It became the body of men and not the body of Christ. It can only be about Jesus and Him alone. We have no title or position but are to be servants only, like when Jesus washed the disciples' feet.

> *"You call Me Teacher and Lord; and you are right, for so I am. If I then, the Lord and the Teacher, washed your feet, you also ought to wash one another's feet. For I gave you an example that you also should do as I did to you. Truly, truly, I say to you, a slave is not greater than his master, nor is one who is sent greater than the one who sent him"* (John 13:13-16)

Jesus said our goals could only be to worship Him and to seek the lost with His Good News. Once we begin to put layers of man's organization and self-important titles and positions into the equation, we leave the simple and faithful work of the Lord! Our goal cannot and must not be to climb the denominational ladder of success. Even if we try to mix the two –the ladder of success and serving Jesus -- we fail.

> Jesus said, *"The greatest among you must be a servant" (Matthew 23:11 NLT).*

> *"Because of the privilege and authority God has given me, I give each of you this warning: Don't think you are better than you really are. Be honest in your evaluation of yourselves, measuring yourselves by the faith God has given us" (Romans 12:3 NLT).*

We must not become Revelation's Ephesian church: being great at church work and yet losing the first love of Jesus. Even today, we must carry the first excitement of our own salvation and let that be the driving force of the work we do. It is the excitement of the cross, forgiveness of our sin, the release of our guilt, and the hope of eternal life that must be the essence of our hearts and work. We must never lose the awe of Jesus allowing us **to serve in His Church**, especially remembering the sinful life we came from and the struggle for holiness we battle every day.

> *"'I know your deeds and your toil and perseverance, and that you cannot tolerate evil men, and you put to the test those who call themselves apostles, and they are not, and you found them to be false; and you have perseverance and have endured for My name's sake, and have not grown weary.*
>
> ***But I have this against you, that you have left your first love. Therefore remember from where you have fallen, and repent and do the deeds you did at first;*** *or else I am coming to you and will remove your lampstand out of its place—unless you repent"* (Revelation 2:2-5).

Pastor Lachica was looking for fellowship and encouragement from likeminded pastors to seek and save the lost. We soon found we had a common goal. At age 59, Pastor Lachica had asked the Lord to let him be able to plant five more churches before He calls him home. At 62, when we met, he had already planted three. After more than a year of fellowship with his three churches and ours, we joined forces to help each other in the service of our Lord.

ANINI-Y CHURCH

Pastor Lachica, with the help of a seed family in Anini-y, was able to start a Bible study in the most southern barangay of our Antique Province. However, Pastor Lachica had no help to pastor the other three churches. He was stretched too thin.

A recovering pastor who previously fell from ministry traveled through Anini-y several times per week. We meet with him and all seemed well and good. However, we learned several months later that he had a mistress traveling with him. She also attended the Anini-y Bible study with him. As you can imagine, the scandal was huge. Sometimes impatience keeps us from good decisions. We should have investigated the pastor more and waited upon the Lord.

During this time, Pastor Lachica had been able to appoint a part-time pastor in one of the other churches, Victory Christian Church Durog Iguirindon. We had talked Pastor Lachica and Teodora into going to Anini-y before, but because they were getting older, the family wanted them to stay in their current home almost two hours from Anini-y. Also, Pastor Lachica's daughter, Teoan Francisco, was now teaching at one of the other churches. She is a high school teacher and raised in the church. The Lachicas taught their children well in worship and in the scriptures. Teoan teaches under the authority and supervision of her father. The church there in Barangbang is primarily mothers, children and youth. It is in a small community that is so thankful to have a church building and Teoan there to teach and pastor the community. Pastor Lachica and Teodora visit when they can.

Well, it became apparent that Anini-y was going to need a full time pastor. The seed host family were evangelizing and they had many youth starting to attend. Without a pastor, they would soon lose them. The seed family had donated land to build a church building. We received a grant from one of our donors to construct a church. We now had a salary available for a pastor. Everything was in place, with the exception of the pastor. One of the problems for the new church was trust after the previous pastor. It was up to God now. He had made everything ready except to show who the pastor was going to be.

Pastors Alagos, Jojo, and I had rehearsed an appeal for the Lachicas to accept an appointment and move to Anini-y. The community loved and respected them. They could heal the hurts and mistrust. Youth love them! They could easily oversee the construction. But would they move from their home at their age, now 65? Would their children allow them to relocate and move so far from them? It was in God's hands now. We were praying, fasting, and waiting on Him with hopeful expectation.

The day came for Juliana and me to pay the Lachicas a visit and see what God would do. We arrived and were greeted with warmth and hospitality, which was their custom. I must have appeared nervous. I barely got the proposal out of my month and Pastor Lachica said, "Yes, we will go!"

I said, "What? Don't you need to discuss this with Teodora and the family?" Pastor Lachica said they had decided sometime back that wherever we would send them they were ready and willing to go. They were ready to start a new life in a new community. I should say now that at this time we were also talking about starting two new churches on other islands. So they had considered all the options in their decision.

The Lachicas at age 65 were ready to go wherever we sent them with no hesitation. Their family and children were in support of the new ministry. Thank you, Lord! He had prepared the hearts of the Anini-y pastors. All was ready and in place with the leading of our Lord, Jesus.

The Anini-y church is happy and thriving. The youth come nearly every night after school to learn instruments and practice worship. It is a healthy church with young, old, and children. The youth of all our Panay churches love to go there for overnight learning and worship. I consider the Lachicas an appointment from our Lord. They are both 67 years of age now, healthy and full of vigor in their service to our God. Please keep them in your prayers.

> *"The righteous will flourish like palm trees; they will grow like a cedar in Lebanon. Planted in the LORD's Temple, they will flourish in the courtyard of our God. They will still bear fruit even in old age; they will be luxuriant and green. They will proclaim: "The LORD is upright; my rock, in whom there is no injustice" (Psalms 92:12-15).*

Anini-y Church

Pastor Antonio and Teodora Lachica Jr.

AMERICAN CATASTROPHES

October 10ᵗʰ, 2017
Hurricanes Harvey, Nate, Irma, Maria, and the horrific wildfires in America

God Is Our Fortress
*"God is our refuge and strength, **A very present help in trouble**.*

Therefore we will not fear, though the earth should change And though the mountains slip into the heart of the sea;

Though its waters roar and foam, Though the mountains quake at its swelling pride. Selah"
(Psalm 46:1-3).

IT HAS NOT BEEN EASY FOR ME TO WATCH FROM AFAR the terrible disasters that have befallen my country and fellow citizens. Some of my dear friends have been directly affected by both the hurricanes and wildfires. My heart and prayers continue for you all. I have written in this book about our experience with Super Typhoon Yolanda here in the Philippines. I know firsthand the tragedy of disaster.

So, in light of THE ENEMY IS ROARING AND GOD IS BLESSING, these are my thoughts and prayers.

I. God Is Sovereign

As followers of Jesus Christ, we must always remember that whatever the reasons may be, God is sovereign – ALWAYS! God is good and He is just – ALWAYS! In tragedy, disease, death, joy, victory, and triumph, God is in control with His sovereignty, goodness, and justice. It was the Lord Jesus Christ who said, *"I have told you all this so that you may have peace in Me. Here on earth you will have many trials and sorrows. But take heart, because I have overcome the world"* (John 16:33 NLT). Thank you, Lord, that we can run for shelter in You, that we can take refuge in You, and we can trust You!

II. No other gods

These things are certain.

- These are NO acts of "Mother Nature." There is no mother over the earth or her nature. There is only God's creation. Only God is Lord over His creation.
- These are NO acts of a "Natural Order." There is NO natural law or order. There is only God's law and His order over His creation and man.

- There are NO Natural Disasters. These things are not ordered or caused by the earth or nature. Only God controls the earth.
- There is NO chaos. There is NO luck or coincidence. **Only God has purpose and design for EVERYTHING!**

These hypotheses become the gods or faith systems of those who refuse to acknowledge God. He is the God of all creation: the absolute sovereign God of all. There is only one God. There are NO other causes and effects, ruling systems, gods, or laws. There is only God and His purpose, His authority, His sovereignty. His is LORD over all and He does not share His divinity.

III. Understanding God

Nevertheless, we who acknowledge God have a hard time understanding the whys and wherefores of such calamities as these. We are not God. Our finite minds cannot fathom the mind of God or His reasoning. All we can do is trust God because we KNOW He is good and just, especially when we do not know the reasons why or when events are beyond our understanding.

Therefore

*"**Trust in the LORD** with all your heart And
do not lean on your own understanding"
(Proverbs 3:5).*

Because we cannot understand, we trust. We live by
and understand by faith. Even in suffering we thank God
that we can hope in Him; we can pray with expectation,
knowing that He loves us and will see us through.

> *"And we know that God causes all things to
> work together for good to those who love God,
> to those who are called according to His pur-
> pose" (Romans 8:28).*

> *"My soul, wait in silence for God only, **For my
> hope is from Him**. He only is my rock and
> my salvation, My stronghold; I shall not be
> shaken. On God my salvation and my glory
> rest; The rock of my strength, my refuge is in
> God. **Trust in Him at all times, O people**;
> Pour out your heart before Him; God is a refuge
> for us. Selah" (Psalm 62:5-8).*

The Enemy Is Roaring

The enemy, Satan, uses EVERYTHING to blame and
accuse God, and to try to diminish or tear down the very

nature of God: His goodness, His justice, His compassion, His love for us. The great question or accusation is "Why would a loving God allow such suffering?" Indeed these hurricanes and fires cause a great deal of death and suffering. The "blame God question" automatically judges God as evil in nature: without goodness, justice, compassion, and love.

I believe we are at the end of this age. The coming of our Lord is imminent. The Bible says that these catastrophic events will increase because our world is dying and ready to meet judgement.

Jesus was asked this question:

> *"Tell us, when will these things happen, and what will be* **the sign of Your coming, and of the end of the age"** *(Matthew 23:3)?*

Here was His answer:

> *v. 6 "You will be hearing of* **wars and rumors of wars**. *See that you are not frightened, for those things must take place, but that is not yet the end.*

> *v. 7 "For* **nation will rise against nation**, *and* **kingdom against kingdom**, *and in various places there will be* **famines and earthquakes.**

*v. 8 "But all these things are **merely the beginning of birth pangs**"*

v. 9 "Then they will deliver you to tribulation, and **will kill you**, and you will be **hated by all nations because of My name**" *(Mathew 24:6-8).*

I am not an "End Times" prophet. However, even a blind man can see these speak directly to our time. Our world is in the *birth pangs* of the *end of our age.* We have had bad weather, earthquakes, and famines always in earth's history, but I believe the intensity and frequency has increased and magnified at the coming of our Lord. He will end this age and the new eternal age will be established.

When He comes, there will be judgement and reward. All those who believe in Him will be rewarded and those who refused Jesus as Savior will be judged. The earth, corrupted with sin, disease, and death, will be judged and destroyed as well. Jesus will destroy it and create a new and perfect world with no sin and death as He did once before. This one is dying and it will soon be gone. That is why the earth is in such turmoil and our governments are in such upheaval. That is why Christians are being killed, beheaded, and tortured in such great number today.

The New Heaven and the New Earth

v. 1 "Then I saw a **new heaven and a new earth; for the first heaven and the first earth passed away,** *and there is no longer any sea.*

v. 2 And I saw the holy city, new Jerusalem, coming down out of heaven from God, made ready as a bride adorned for her husband.

v. 3 And I heard a loud voice from the throne, saying, **"Behold, the tabernacle of God is among men,** *and He will dwell among them, and they shall be His people, and God Himself will be among them,*

v. 4 and **He will wipe away every tear from their eyes; and there will no longer be any death; there will no longer be any mourning, or crying, or pain; the first things have passed away."**

v. 5 And He who sits on the throne said, **"Behold, I am making all things new."** *And He said, "Write, for* **these words are faithful and true"** *(Revelation 21:1-5).*

Judgement and Discipline

God does use weather and systems of the earth for judgement and discipline.

For example,

- When the earth became totally corrupted, God use the great flood to judge and destroy the inhabitants.
- God used seven years of exceptional weather and then seven years of famine to move the nation of Israel to the land of Goshen, Egypt.
- The ten plagues of death, disease, blight, insects, miraculous events of turning water to blood, and darkness for judgments on Egypt and the freeing of Israel.
- God used the Red Sea to bring judgement on Egypt by drowning its army in it.
- God stopped time (the sun and the moon stood still) while He gave victory to Israel. (Joshua 10:13)
- God demonstrated His power and confirmed the man of God Elijah by stopping the rain for three years and restarting it again at Elijah's command.
- The moving of a star to lead the three kings to the birth of Jesus.

Christ's second coming is proclaimed and evidenced by the tragic events of today: we corrupted ourselves and the earth with our sin and rebellion. I believe that judgement and discipline are not only on the world and nations but also on individuals.

THE LORD IS BLESSING

God uses everything available to bring about repentance and salvation. Nothing is more important to God than for each of us to be saved, strengthened, and matured in our saving faith.

He either causes events, works through them, or allows them for His purpose. In tragedy, disease, death, joy, victory, and triumph, God is in control with His sovereignty, goodness, and justice. His purpose is to restore that which is lost through sin and rebellion.

God is our protector, justifier, and provider in our present need.

"But let the godly rejoice. Let them be glad in God's presence. Let them be filled with joy. Sing praises to God and to His name! Sing loud praises to Him who rides the clouds. His name is the LORD—rejoice in His presence! Father to the fatherless, defender of widows— this is God, whose dwelling is holy. God places the lonely in families; He sets the prisoners free and gives them joy. But He makes

the rebellious live in a sun-scorched land. O God, when You led your people out from Egypt, when You marched through the dry wasteland, Interlude.

"The earth trembled, and the heavens poured down rain before You, the God of Sinai, before God, the God of Israel. You sent abundant rain, O God, to refresh the weary land. There Your people finally settled, and with a bountiful harvest, O God, You provided for Your needy people" (Psalm 68:3-10 NLT).

Our hope is in God. We can call upon Him in our day of trouble. When He blesses us in the midst of trouble, it will bring glory to His name!

*"Make thankfulness your sacrifice to God, and keep the vows you made to the Most High. **Then call on Me when you are in trouble, and I will rescue you, and you will give Me glory**" (Psalm 50:15 NLT).*

After Super Typhoon Yolanda came through the Philippines, my prayer was, "God, we have seen what the storm can do. Now show us your great mercy!"

Billions of dollars in aid from all over the world flooded in. Churches, schools, communities, NGOs, and peoples became the blessing and mercies of God.

Our churches more than doubled in size. Many heard the Gospel for the first time, some were reminded, and some repented unto salvation. For numerous people, this could only have come because of the typhoon. It is the same for America and throughout the world.

For we who believe, we have the ear of our Lord Jesus Christ who sits on His magnificent throne of grace. Jesus experienced everything we do. He experienced hunger, heat and cold, homelessness, rejection, a broken heart, false judgement, torture, and death. He knows firsthand our suffering.

Therefore, He invites us to His Throne of Grace to receive His undeserved favor: not because we deserve it, but because He knows and understands our need: because He loves us! In answering our pleas for help, He will bring aid to our suffering, victory to our defeat, justice to our enemies, and glory to His name: Jesus.

Jesus the Great High Priest

"Therefore, since we have a great high priest who has passed through the heavens, Jesus the Son of God, let us hold fast our confession.

For we do not have a high priest who cannot sympathize with our weaknesses, but One who has been tempted in all things as we are, yet without sin.

Therefore **let us draw near with confidence** *to the* **throne of grace***, so that* **we may receive mercy and find grace to help in time of need***" (Hebrews 4:14-16).*

Amen!

CLEAR VISION

"Create in me a clean heart, O God, And renew a steadfast spirit within me. Do not cast me away from Your presence And do not take Your Holy Spirit from me. <u>Restore to me the joy of Your salvation And sustain me with a willing spirit</u>" (Psalm 51:10-12).

RECENTLY, I SPENT A MONTH OF PRAYER AND PERI-odic fasting, seeking the Lord. Psalm 51:10-12 was my focused prayer.

I am happy to report that shortly thereafter, my heart filled with restored confidence and faith in my Lord. I was like Peter when he began to walk on the sea and then took his eyes off the Lord and saw the storm and the wind and waves and he began to sink. My sabbatical month's goal was to see the Lord again in my life.

I renewed my thinking and faith that this is His ministry; His responsibility; His harvest – not mine! I am seeing myself again as a servant, not a leader. If it is not God Who shines through me, then it is time to go home.

After the month of prayer and fasting, I had a wonderful daydream -- or maybe it was a vision.

I was sitting by a swimming pool while our Grace Chapel youth group enjoyed themselves in the pool. Then suddenly it hit me that if Juliana and Steven and I were not here, there would no youth group. The kids sang songs to our Lord about His love and power in their lives as they swam. What a blessing!

Then, in my mind's eye, I saw all the faces of the people that worship at Grace Chapel. These were fruits of this ministry. Then I saw the worshipers at Anini-y, Esparar, Calapadan, Mabasa, and Igbarawan. I saw each church's worship service and observed each person. They were all smiling and singing to the Lord.

What a wonderful blessing from our Lord – He was showing me how my life fits in His purpose. My life is not in vain. Thank you, Lord.

This is why I was born. This why I am here.

This is also one of the reasons for your life!

EACH OF YOU WITH YOUR LOVE, PRAYER, AND SUPPORT HAVE MADE ALL THIS HAPPEN. SO MANY LIVES HAVE BEEN SAVED – SO MANY LIVES HAVE BEEN CHANGED – SO MANY STORIES ABOUT PEOPLE'S LIVES HAVE BEEN WRITTEN WITH GLORY TO GOD.

Together with our Lord's blessing, we are making a difference!

Thank You, Lord, for this wonderful pleasure. Thank you all for this joyous blessing!

Your partner in the Philippines ministry,

Pastor Steven Ray Bragg

Grace Chapel Youth at the Swim

ENDNOTES

1   https://medium.com/@mattflorence/who-are-the-new-peoples-army-of-the-philippines-8c6c2dac9871

2   http://www.caremin.com/contact-us

3   http://www.riseagainsthunger.org/

4   https://harvestpack.org/

CPSIA information can be obtained
at www.ICGtesting.com
Printed in the USA
LVHW05s2004040618
579543LV00013B/66/P